Lady Lumberjack

Dorothea Mitchell at Silver Mountain

by Dorothea Mitchell

SILVER MOUNTAIN
PUBLISHING

Publisher: Silver Mountain Publishing,
3065 Hwy 588 R.R. #2 Nolalu,
Silver Mountain, ON, Canada P0T 2K0.
Designer: Michael OReilly (HelpLink.com Communications)

Library and Archives Canada Cataloguing in Publication
ISBN No. 9780991776504

Mitchell, Dorothea, 1877-1976, author
Lady Lumberjack / Dorothea Mitchell.

Originally published: Vancouver : Mitchell Press, 1967.
Includes bibliographical references and index.
ISBN 97809917765-0-4 (pbk.)

1. Mitchell, Dorothea, 1877-1976. 2. Pioneers--Ontario, Northern--Biography. 3. Women loggers--Ontario, Northern--Biography.
4. Frontier and pioneer life--Ontario,Northern.
I. Title.

FC3094.25.M58A3 2013 971.3è103092   C2013-901946-4

Contents

Dedication and Acknowledgements   4
Foreward   5

Westward Go!   6
Anything Can Happen   12
Cash Money and Venture   19
Headed for the Boundary   28
Adventure in Cordwood   36
Paddy Reappears   42
Contract with Queer Angles   46
I Buy Timber   53
A Spinster Homesteads   59
The Family Arrives   67
Photos   75
Game-Wardens and Spotters   82
The Musical Dog   88
Unpremeditated Acquistion   93
Volunteer School and Cookstove Camera   100
Let's Have Eggs for Supper!   105
Fate, Fruit and Fire   110
What Next?   116
Another Fire   122
Production Starts Again   127
Camp Cook   134
The Later Years   142
Appendix   153

Silver Mountain Rises   155

This book is dedicated to

Elinor Barr
and
Elle Andra-Warner

Their mentorship, support and continual friendship made this book possible. Meeting them both was truly unexpected; they have both become a valued and significant part of my life since moving here to Silver Mountain.

A special thanks to Elle-Andra-Warner for her continued work and support for the reprint of this book.

Shelley Simon
September 20, 2013

Foreward

In a lifetime now exceeding slightly the allotted three score and ten, I have known many doughty and indomitable personalities, but to none of them do I concede any greater courage, initiative and strength of character than I do to the author of this book – whom I have been priviliged to know since the early 1920s.

That she has taken up her pen to write the story of her experiences is only one more demonstration of that spirit of pioneering that has governed her whole life and while, at the moment of inscribing this Foreword, I have not had the opportunity of reading her story, I am sure it will have been written with that complete fidelity and integrity so characteristic of her.

Not only that, but I am certain that the imagination of her readers will be captured by the force and vitality of her saga and that they will not rest until they have met the author when, to their surprise, they will face, not a female Paul Bunyan – if such there be – but a gracious, charming and completely feminine writer whose personality almost belies the truth of the story she has told.

And so, Lady Lumberjack, may an old friend – in turn the son of a "lumberjack" -- salute you for your worthy accomplishment in the field of literature and commend your book unreservedly as an absorbing narrative of work and adventure in the woods of Northern Ontario.

July 5th, 1966
R. Lloyd Seaman, Q.C.
Port Arthur, Ontario.

CHAPTER ONE

Westward Go!

S trange, isn't it, how a few printed words can change the whole trend of a person's life? The advertisement read: "Desired, an educated young woman as Companion-help to Superintendent's wife in mining camp, N.W. Ontario. Some office duties."

Was this my opportunity? It had been something of an adventure for me to come to Canada (in my 20's) to ''try out'' the country for the rest of the family – a widowed mother and sister. After five years in Toronto and Hamilton, Mother, who had ben paying me an extended visit, planned shortly to return to England, leaving me free to follow that urge for the West. Not very far west, I'll admit, but even 900-odd miles was not too bad – for a start.

Telephoning the Toronto address, I made an appointment for an interview the following day. I liked both my prospective employers. They didn't seem to feel my lack of office experience detrimental, and a date was set for my arrival at Silver Mountain in the Lakehead area.

After spending a night in Port Arthur, I boarded the ''local'', a mixed train that took six hours to do the 40-mile run, stopping at noon to allow passengers to regate themselves at a village boarding-house.

By the platform at Silver Mountain Station stood a team of heavy bush horses and novel sleigh: two sets of huge runners, chained to which were several two-inch planks, the driver's seat being a bale of hay. The teamster, a most extraordinary looking individual, was presented to me by the Superintendent as Timothy Naylor. A burly speciment, bundled up in heavy mackinaw garments, a grey wool cap dragged down over both ears, a scraggy grizzled beard and whiskers, the general effect was nicely topped off by one over-sized black eye ("shiner", I subsequently learned, was the correct caption). But what intrigued me most was a little row of icicles dangling from his moustache! The horses had them, too, from their nostrils. This, also, was a ''first'' for me... the freezing of breath.

Inviting me to share the bale of hay, Tim carefully tucked a horse-blanket – a very *horsy* horse-blanket – around my knees. I mentally dubbed the gentleman "the grizzly bear''. My baggage was loaded to the rear. The trunk, being fortunately of the flattop variety, served as a convenient seat for the mine Superintendent. A mile and a quarter, mostly up-grade, brought us to the camp, very picturesquely spread over the mountain side. The two-storey office building had also a huge storage space and furance-room on the ground floor, with excellent living quarters above. One of the first things that really surprised me, when being shown over the latter, was a large bath-room with modern plumbing. "Imagine such a thing!" I exclaimed. "Such a distance from civilization." The second surprise was that the bath-tub was full of cold water. This called for a somewhat lengthy explanation. "During summer months both hot and cold water are supplied by the pump-house; but, since piples are laid above ground which sometimes freezes to a depth of six feet, they are naturally useless in winter. This means that water has to be carried some distance up the hill from an excellent well every day and dumped into the bath-tub for general use.'' Hot water was obtained by favor of the cook-stove, necessitating the use of a mere sitz-bath until the arrival of spring.

Although refraining from voicing my feelings, I'll admit to disappointment in the general terrain. A map of the district showed lakes dotted around the area, and I had

noted numerous rivers and creeks during the journey up.
Possibly the very name Silver Mountain had conjured up
a mental picture of greater ruggedness. At that time, I had
not been through the Rockies, nor up Mount Washburn
in Wyoming; but I had journeyed up the Western Ghats
in India – seven hours on horseback, from railway to the
summit. So what were here termed mountains seemed like
nice little hills, usually steep, sometimes precipitous, on
one side, but not hard to climb.

Across the road was the boarding house, operated by a
Norwegian and his German wife, where lesser executives
lived and meals were provided for unmarried miners whose
bunkhouse was some distance away. Farther up the hill
were the shaft-house, enginerooms, stamp mill (on four
levels) and compressor. Scattered around between these
various buildings were picturesque log cabins for married
men with families. Quite the larger proportion of miners
(possibly 70 in all) were Italian, some Austrian and a few
Polish. Yes, we were truly cosmopolitan!

To one who had lived only in cities since coming to
this country, life in the mining camp was full of interest
and intrigue. So far, the term ''unorganized territory'' had
conveyed little to me and I admit to a feeling of apart-ness
when informed we had neither the services of a doctor,
clergy nor police within forty miles. Our railway, a branch
line of the C.N.R., favoured us with three trains per week of
the ''mixed'' variety, indicating passenger, mail, wayfreight
and logging. Full title was the Port Arthur, Duluth and
Western – locally referred to as the Pee Dee. It was older
than the main-line going West. It never did connect with
Duluth, the United States having failed to complete its
construction to Gunflint on their side of the International
boundary.

The stamp-mill possibly interested me most. The

freshly mined rock would be trammed out in small mine
cars pushed by a husky miner after being raised from the
depths by the mainshaft cage (elevator), then trundled
across an aerial track to the top level of the stamp-mill and
dumped into the crusher bin. After crushing, it was dropped
through to a lower level, where it was further crushed
and ground until by the time it had passed through four
levels the material was reduced to the consistency of sand.
Next came the washing. On ground level were nine huge
vanners, each equipped with a revolving (almost level)
rubber belt, about seven feet wide and ten long, over which
flowed a constant stream of water. The ground ore came
down into this stream, the non-metallic sand being washed
away and the valuable material now ready for shipment to
the smelter.

On several occasions I was asked to accompany
members of the staff when out to shoot birds or rabbits.
Once I was handed a shot-gun, with the whispered words:

"See if you can get that patridge."

"I'm sure I can't; it's directly behind a sapling!"

"Well, try anyway."

Much to my astonishment, I not only got the bird,
but cut off the sapling also. One of them said, rather
accusingly: "This is not the first time you've handled a
gun!"

"No. But that was at the age of nine, when an uncle
who lived with us in Bombay taught us all, with a pistol
mounted in a home-made stock, to aim at a target – in the
compound."

I'd never dreamed I'd have the heart to kill anything,
so it was quite a shock. However, when later ''on my own''
finidng that, without refrigeration, we completlely lacked
fresh meat during the summer months, my qualms had
to be overcome. I bought myself a single-barrle shot-gun

(double was too heavy for a woman), which earned for
me a bit of a reputation; but that was only because I'd a
horror of maiming anything – and having it get away in that
condition. Unless pretty certain of getting my quarry, I did
not fire. In any event, I made a a practice of aiming above
the head – the surest way to hit or miss. Single barrels are
noted for having a tremendous ''kick'', which seemed to
discourage neighbours from asking to borrow it a second
time. One man said it gave him a black eye; another that,
after firing in one direction, he ended up facing in the
opposite!

Another thing that astonished me was that men of
limited education could become efficient and trusted
assistant engineers, handling the essential and costly
equipment. Regulations governing such tings were then
lacking, I imagine. One, a sturdy little man in his thirties,
was in charge of the pumping station supplying water
to the entire plant. It was a lonesome job, the source of
supply being a small lake on top of another hill, separated
from the mine by a deep gully. But Tommy was ambitious;
in leisure moments he was teaching himself to read and
write. Incidentially, the first letter he ever attempted was
addressed to me.

The second was an Irish-Canadian named Billy, who
with wife and four half-savage children lived close by.
The first time I saw him ascending the stairs to speak to
the Superintendent I thought he must be a negro – tall,
with black beard and hair and an exceptionally dusky
complexion, reminiscent of Robinson Crusoe. At a later
date he confided to me that he never washed his face
between October and spring thaw – "It's warmer this way."
And judging by the look of his home and children, his wife
shared the logic.

Number three was an Englishman, Saxby, evidently a

man with some background but heartily disliked because he was forever boasting of his personal achievements, notably the fact that he had ''hoofed it'' entirely across Canada, and had the signature of every station agent to prove it!

Last but not least came Paddy O'Connor, a full-blooded Irishman, and quite the most interesting of the lot, possessing the charming brogue and silvery tongue capable of coaxing blood from a stone and of generally ''getting away with murder''. Paddy was lean and angular. Earlier in his life he'd been a contortionist in a circus ''on the owld sod'' but had been obliged to chane his occupation on account of a back injury. One evening we heard considerable shouting and commotion between camp buildings. Presently a foreman came to the Superintendent's quarters to report that Paddy, anxious to entertain off-duty miners, had been doing some of his funny-stuff of circus days and had become tied up in knots from which he could not extricate himself. At first they thought this was part of the show, but eventually he had to have help. Obviously he was not partially paralyzed. Next morning, poor Paddy was conveyed on a stretcher to the railway station, thence by train to a city hospital where he made a slow recovery and did not return to the mine.

CHAPTER TWO

Anything Can Happen

One of my self-imposed duties was to meet the tri-weekly train and collect the mail. The walk never became monotonous, aspects changing so entirely with varying seasons.

One particularly lovely spring day – the air balmy, birds twittering, here and there a partridge ''drumming'', rabbits skitttering out of the way because the snow was gone and their coats were still white – I thought, ''the whole world is at peace''.

Having been asked to look out for a stranger, relative of one of our officials, who was expected on the train for a brief visit, I made a point of starting early, the local being just as liable to arrive twenty minutes ahead of time, as two hours late! I'd hardly seated myself on the wooden bench outside the ticket-office window and became interested in the activities of a river-drivers' camp across the track, when the station agent hurried out and said in imploring tones, "Oh, please come inside!"

"No, thanks! I'd much rather sit out here, Mr. Haggarty."

A nervous little man at the best of times, he was by now literally hopping from one foot to the other. "I beg of you!'' So entered the waiting-room. "There's something I must tell you," he continued. "Do you know, you almost sat down in a pool of blood."

That would, admittedly, have been unpleasant, but hardly warranted such tragic tones. Then, in jerks and splutters, out came the story. It was not difficult – knowing the people involved and something of their characteristics –

to piece together the story.

In the locality lived two veterans of the Boer War, real pals living about two miles apart, and ''batching''. Murdo was very definitely ''bushed'' at times and knowing this the young sons of his nearest neighbour teased him as opportunity offered. When one of these seizures overcame Murdo, he would place chairs in a semi-circle in his shack, drape blankets over (forming an imaginery trench), grasp his rifle and hide behind this barracade, awaiting the enemy.

On the previous evening, when duly entrenched, there came a knock at the door and instantly he fired, straight through it. The visitor was his best friend and South African buddy, Al Barton, whose right elbow was shattered by the 30-30 bullet.

Staggering from the shock and pain, the injured man made his way to the neighbour's farm (whose boys had indirectly been the cause of the calamity) seeking help. Mrs. Jorgen had never heard of such a contrivance as a tourniquet, so filled the wound with flour! She insisted also that the house be kept in complete darkness, lest a lighted window prove a target for Murdo's irresponsible aim. Of the happenings during the long hours of the night, nobody ever obtained a lucid picture, though one of the elder boys carried the news to the railway station soon after day-break.

A couple of hours later Murdo himself, barefoot, set off in the same direction, rifle in hand. Arrived at the station, he seated himself on the aforementioned bench. News of the events of the previous night had naturally reached the river-drivers' camp. One of the younger men decided he'd better relieve Murdo of his weapon, so he strolled casually towards the building. It didn't work! Instantly, the rifle was aimed at him. The young chap was not so easily daunted. Taking a circuitous route through the bush and behind buildings, he darted around the corner of the statin and grabbed the rifle. Not, however, before Murdo had pulled the trigger with his great toe, cutting a furrow in his own temple, the bullet continuing up through the overhanging roof. Thus was Haggarty's ''pool of blood'' accounted for.

Perfectly docile without his weapon, Murdo had been taken over to the boarding-house, there to await transportation to the city. All this had happened shortly before my arrival on the station platform. Had I made an earlier appearance, quite possibly I would have been shot!

The guest expected on the train had, I knew, been a Surgeon's mate in the Royal Navy. Directly I told him of Barton's plight, he volunteered to go out to the Jorgen farm, dress the wounded arm and supervise conveyance of the patient to the track. The train Conductor promised to stop at a convenient spot and pick them up when returning, two hours later.

Thus these two buddies – Murdo and Barton – journeyed to the city together and entered the same hospital, Murdo later being admitted to a mental institution.

Wending my way back to the mine with the mail, I came to the conclusion the world was not quite so happy and carefree a place as had been indicated earlier in the day by bird, beast and balmy weather.

Then came excitement of another sort. I'd been at the mines seven or eight months and it was mid-summer – season for bush fires, I was told – but so far there had been none in our immediate neighbourhood. This being another ''first'' for me, I climbed to the top of the mountain, where one could reconnoitre in every direction. Within a distance of a few miles, I counted eleven conflagratons, none of which looked serious.

One day, however, heavy clouds of thin smoke began to drift from the South. There was no means of knowing precisely what this indicated until the next train brought newspapers telling of fires raging in Northern Minnesota, one small town having been completely wiped out; fires consuming valuable timber were out of control.

Gradually smoke became denser, then white ash – like snowflakes – began to descent; we realy thought we were in for it! Fortunately, running water was available. All work stopped except the pumps keeping the mine itself dry. Every available man, and even I, was assigned a hose-station, mine on the roof of the office building. No one undressed for two nights. If we slept, it was ''with one eye open'', expecting the alarm.

Mercifully, the fires burned out before reaching us, but for a whole month the sun was invisible, except as a molten ball showing through a pall of smoke. And for a whole month, not a drop of alleviating rain!

It appeared that most of the neighbourhood homesteaders had, at one time or another, lost their dwellings, there being no means of fire-fighting except by bucket brigade from a nearby well or creek. When this happened, everyone would chip in to build a new home – a wonderful spirit! But loss of personal possessions must have caused heartbreak.

One the whole, my duties were proving lighter than anticipated. It was, however, something of a shock to find that the wife of the Superintendent, who obviously was not interested in primitive surroundings, spent more time in Toronto and Ottawa than at the mine! This naturally threw considerably more responsibility upon me, including the entertainment of various official visitors from the city who had to remain two days until the next train. (Roads were not yet fit for automobiles.) I found time, however, in which to explore the district and to learn something of varied processes involved before the silver ore was ready for shipment. I also taught myself to use an ancient typewriter known as a *Yost,* a make I had never heard of.

Both underground and surface foremen were Italian, speaking good English. Few of the miners, though, knew more than very simple words; names were specially difficult for them to remember. They called the Superintendent ''Head Man'' and the Chief Engineer "Big Boss''. Thinking the appellations rather ingenious, we soon adopted the habit in the office.

One day our chore-man came stumbling up the stairs in a state of excitement, saying repeatedly ..... "I loos-a ma pail! I loos-a ma pail! Big Boss he be mad!" Finally, by piecing his scrappy explation together, it was evident that the pail with which he drew water from the well had detached itself from the rope and remained at the bottom. I promptly took him to the storeroom and gave him another pail and a new length of rope. From then on, he was my devoted slave!

Weeks went rapidly by until Christmas was approaching. One day Tommy (he of the pumping-station) – who happened to be the elder son of the people who owned the local hostelry near the track – tendered me a polite ''invite'' to a party being given by his Mother on Christmas Eve, at the same time mentioning he owned a horse and cutter and would be glad to convey me ''to and from same''.

Dolly was a nervous animal at the best of times. Having only one eye, she was inclined to shy at imaginary objects on the blind side of the road. The evening of the party, Tommy said she was more jumpy than usual; but it was not until later it was found that someone with a perverted sense of humour had loosened all the harness buckles and tied things together with light twine. By the time we reached the last steep down-grade, the poor brute must have felt the cutter bumping against her hind legs, for she simply bolted for home.

Bush parties always took the form of a dance. Everyone within a radius of several miles was expected to attend, younger children being put to bed and older ones allowed to look on, not to dance. In this case, the room was large and minus furniture except for a huge box-stove and benches all around the whitewashed log walls. The floor, well scrubbed for the occasion, was ''pocked'' by years of frequenters wearing calked boots, but rendered comparatively smooth by a liberal springing of corn-starch.

The orchestra consisted of a squeaky fiddle and a mouth organ, Tommy acting as ''caller''. In due course he shouted:

"Pick up your partners for a square-dance!"

From then on, I couldn't understand one word he said, therefore did not attempt to join the happy throng. Everyone danced with great gusto – "pranced" is perhaps a more fitting word – while I sat there enjoying the novel scene and hoping nobody resented my obvious amusement. An older gent asked: "Don't you have square-dancing in England?" to which I replied, "Oh, yes. We have Quadrilles and Lancers, but everyone knows the set. We are not told what to do. That is what seems so funny."

Naturally I sized up the deportment and dance-style of the motley crowd, and was somewhat impressed by a six-foot man of wiry build, well-dressed and probably fifty, who had not as yet been introduced. Some business man from the city, merely here over-night, I thought.

Square-dancing continued well into the night. It was something of a relief when a change was suggested. The tall man came over and asked if I cared to waltz. I accepted and found him an excellent partner.

Later, on our way to the dining room for refreshments, he said, with a sly sort of smile:

"I don't think you recognize me."

"I'm awfully sorry," I replied. "Have we met before?"

"Why, yes, I drove you up to the mines when you arrived from Toronto." (My ''grizzly bear!")

When I complimented him on his dancing, he laughed and said, ''My Ma always said I was born to dance; said I tried to do steps before I could walk. It must be the Scot in me!"

It appeared that Tim had a partner, Jake Blackie, and they had contracted to supply our silver mine with two thousand cords of wood, the only fuel available. Later I was told that, though an expert in every branch of the timber business, Tim could neither read nor write, Jake looking after contracts and financing.

CHAPTER THREE

Cash Money and Venture

I wonder how many readers will have enjoyed the experience of involvement in a strike? By this I don't mean being ''on strike'' yourselves – just connected with the executive end of things.

The fascinating aspect of life in the mining camp was that something was always happening. This West End mine was a one-time ''Bonanza'', second richest in the district and discovered by Oliver Dunais [Daunais] towards the end of the nineteenth century. Recently it had been purchased by a Toronto company and certain changes in staff had been deemed advisable. The new Superintendent who impressed me as more of a stock broker than metallurgist started by discharging the Chief Engineer, a personable young man with plenty of ambition but reputed to be a graduate of a correspondence course and without previous practical experience. Since Arthur was part Italilan – and a large number of the employees were of that nationality – there was a ''feeling'' in the camp, and it was not very long before we felt the impact of it!

The new Chief, an exceptionally fine man, was not only an expert in stationary but in marine engineering, having in earlier years served as an officer in the Royal Navy.

Our Head Office was in Toronto. At the end of each month it was customary for me to make up the time-sheets and mail them East, the resulting pay-cheques being back by the 15th of the ensuing month – the accepted practice for concerns of this sort. However, the price of silver was dropping and the rich ore apparently beginning to peter out. Old Carlotti, the underground foreman, speaking of the principal vein, would say disgustedly: "She don't go up. She don't go down. She must go somewhere – son of a gun!". The executives felt worried, but kept their feelings to themselves.

In short, the mine was not paying. The man who held a controlling interest in the company dipped into his own pocket on several occasions to keep things going, rather than issue more stock. Then came a financial slow-up; pay-cheques didn't arrive on time; the men grumbled and worked half-heartedly. We in the office were sympathetic but could do nothing. Later came the time when cheques arrived but were dishonoured. That was a little too much! In future the men wanted ''cash money''.

The Superintendent hurried to Toronto. Head Office said it should be as the men wished. But by the 15 th of the month, no cash had arrived and everything came to a standstill. That is, the miners and foremen quit; engineers realized that if the pumps stopped, allowing the mine to flood, there wouldn't be work for anyone.

Days passed uneventfully. Groups of miners wandered aimlessly around the camp or on the road to the station. Then one day, returning with the mail, I noticed a young stranger walking ahead of me, carrying a case of whiskey on his shoulder. This, I later found out, was Arthur, the former Enginer-in-charge. Everyone in the district knew it was strictly illegal to sell whiskey within a three-mile radius of any mining camp. But Arthur wasn't selling it; he was just intent on giving his old pals a good time, incidentally causing dissension between two factions. Not until I lived among them did I realize the antagonism existing between Northern and Southern Italians. While apparently getting along amicably at work, they would not think of mixing '''socially''.

Naturally I knew nothing of what transpired the

eveining of Arthur's arrival, but next day heard that Luigi, the engineer had managed to hopelessly tangle the cable which hoists the cage (lift). This, I might say, occurred when men worked 12-hour shifts, and it happened that the young Englishman, Saxby, came on duty at 7.00 a.m. next day. He had either refrained from or had not been invited to join in the celebrations, probably the latter, owing to his unpopularity.

About the middle of the afternoon, Big Boss (acting now as Superintendent) came to me and said, ''Saxby was as mad as blazes when he went on duty this morning and found the cable in such a mess and I can't blame him. But he is threatening to take it out on Luigi when they change shifts. If I go up it'll look obvious. Saxby is twice the size of Luigi, and I'm honestly scared of what may happen. I wonder if you'd stroll up there around 6.45, and get him going on his hiking topic?".

"Sure!" I said. "He's half expecting me anyway, because I promised to go up one of these days, and learn how to work the hoist."

Following up on my interest in machinery I spent a good deal of my spare time in the various buildings, learning how things wree done – stamp-mill, shaft-house, boiler-room and even down the mine – so Saxby was not suspicious. After showing me the tangled cable he said he hadn't the least intention of trying to fix it unaided (it didn't matter anyway, since while the strike lasted nobody was using the hoist). I steered the conversation to the subject of his memorable hike. This put him in a good humour and he escorted me back to the residence instead of ''doing in'' poor Luigi. The ruse had worked!

Each mail day, as I left for the post office, Big Boss would say, ''You won't forget to drop over to the station, will you, and see if that express package has arrived? If it has, I'll go down for it later."

After several such calls and negative responses, the Agent beckoned me into his office. "It's come – and I hope it won't be left overnight!".

"No chance," was my reply. "The Boss told me he'd be down for it later, though I know he doesn't like leaving the camp while this strike is on.   I wonder if I should take it? I will if you can lend me a revolver – just in case. It will save another half-day's idleness."

He hesitated. "Yes, I have a revolver, but no cartridges."

"That won't make any difference. Who's to know whether it's loaded or not?". Taking it from a drawer, he handed it to me in a gingerly manner, remarking, "I'm a bit nervous of firearms myself."

The express package was quite heavy, containing coin as well as bills of varying denomination, totally several thousand dollars. Dumping it in the bottom of the mailbag, and the mail on top, I slung it over my shoulder. On the way home I passed several groups of miners. Each either greeted me or touched his cap. So ended our strike.

Towards fall a general feeling of unrest was again apparent in the camp, brought about possibly by the extended absence of the Head Man; neither did any word come from him. Only Big Boss and I were aware that, owing to a serious drop in the value of silver, the mine was not paying. We half expected orders to shut down. With a second and probably much serious strike looming in the near future, the Big Boss decided he must go to Toronto for a show-down with officials of the company.

"Do you think yu can handle things for a few day?" he asked. "We simply can't go on like this. I'll leave full workorders with the foreman and there's not much likelihood of trouble."

"I'm quite sure there won't be," I replied. "They all

know that you are making the trip on their behalf. I'll have nothing to do but collect the mail and distribute the pay-roll – if it comes!".

And rather to my surprise, it did, and before pay-day, too!

When ready, I told the surface foreman I wanted him with me in the office, and not to allow more than two men in at a time. Once more everyone was happy!

I'd often wondered what had sparked the dismissal of Carlotti, the underground foreman, who had been with the previous owners a considerable time. Then one day I was invited to go on a little exploration jaunt down the mine, being given a cap-lamp for the occasion. Leaving the hoist on one of the lower levels, we followed our leader for some distance along the drift. Suddenly it appeared we were at a sloping dead-end. We scrambled up and found – close to the roof – an aperture, possibly fifteen inches high by three feet wide, sufficient space through which to squeeze on our ''tummies''. Then we slid down a similar slope on the inside.

It was reminiscent of an Aladdin's Cave – minus shimmering jewels! Leaning against the wall wa a long, slim pole, at the top of which a candle was attached (obviously for searching the roof), and by its side a long slender ladder. All around the base of the walls were neatly arranged ore-sacks, full of handpicked ore. Some loyal member of our gang had confided to the Big Boss that this cache had been accumulated by Carlotti, subsequent to the new owners' advent. He had hoped the mine might eventually revert to the original outfit, to whom he apparently felt he owned [owed] allegiance. When shipped, this carload proved of immensely higher assay than any in the past twelve months. Quite a fillip to Head Office! (In those days no Canadian smelter could handle ore of the special type mined at Silver Mountain, so it had to be shipped to Omaha, Nebraska.)

Occasionally, I would be sent to the City (expenses paid) on matters of business for the company. This gave me an opportunity for a little personal shopping and for taking in a show. Sometimes, too, members of the train crew would ask me to visit their wives, several of whom remained my firm friends for many years.

Nearly thirty years later, when I was training in the Canadian Red Cross Transport Corps, the drill sergeant approached me and said, "I remember you! When I worked in the Customs Office, you used to come down from Silver Mountain to clear the car-loads of ore for Nebraska."

Towards the finale, Head Man came West to make exact plans for closing down. He asked me to go to their office in Toronto.

"No, thank you!" was my decided answer. "I like this part of the country better than any city."

"But, Miss Mitchell, there'll be absolutely nothing for you to do! When the mine closes, this place will be dead."

"Perhaps. But if I can't find anything here, I'll go farther west." And that was that!

It transpired that a skeleton crew was to be kept on for a while and my services retained on a half-time basis. This offered an opportunity to look around, and as luck (or fate) would have it, the station agent was just then relieved of his duties, because he was running a little grocery store 'on the side'. After an initial warning he had transferred the business to his wife's name, and persuaded a neighbour to build a small lumber shack on ground adjacent to the railway property. This didn't improve matters, since he had to be over there helping the lady, which brought about the final dismissal.

Then he approached me as a possible buyer. At first I

said, "But I don't know a thing about running a store! I've never been behind a counter, except at a charity bazaar."

After mulling things over I decided that anyone of average intelligence should be able to catch on. A deal was made; I divided my time between office duties at the mine and my little single-board lock-up store near the track. It wasn't altogether satisfactory. In summer everything meltable melted. In winter, everything freezable froze; canned goods containing much liquid (such as tomatoes) would freeze solid overnight. Then, when heat from the stove warmed them up, I'd hear a gentle little ''pop'' as they burst! I paid $5.00 a month rent, too.

Still having living quarters at the mine, I naturally had to walk to and from, in all weather, which wasn't too satisfactory, either.

Also, I was soon to learn that ''cash money'' was as necessary to me as to the miners. My first sizeable customer was their boarding-house keepers. But it wasn't long before they found there were insufficient employees left to make it pay, so they departed rather suddenly, bestowing on me four half-starved hogs and a cow – ''if I could find her'' – in settlement of their debt of $86.00. After three days' hunt, said bovine was located in an abandoned feed-shed, where, scrounging around for food, she had obviously pushed the door shut. After a few weeks of ample feeding, the combined five eralized enough to liquidate the debt.

Even in this funny little venture of mine, there were exciting moments. One very hot afternoon, when there was nothing doing and the door stood wide open, I suddenly caught sight of Tommy (late of the pumping-station) racing full speed in my direction. He dashed in and slammed the door shut, then gasped, breathlessly: "There's a tornado coming! – and if it hits a building with a door open, it'll topple it right over."

In appearance it resembled a sloping pillar of black smoke – possibly gathering up ashes from bush fires. Luckily, it missed us. I'd always associated tornadoes with tropical climates, so this was another ''first'' for me.

On the other side of the track, exactly opposite my little store, was a big barn, housing twelve head of horses; it had double doors. One Friday, in summer, Tim arrived on the local, bringing several friends for a week-end of fishing. Rain was descending in torrents, so to while away the time, they repaired to this barn – accompanied by several cases of beer – and sat in the open doorway. Someone produced a .22 rifle and suggested a contest in marksmanship. They set up shells on the further track (maybe fifteen feet away), then, seated on beercases, aimed at them. Every now and then there'd be a ''ping'' or ''zing'', according to the angle at which the bullet hit the rail. Standing in the doorway, fascinated, I kept thinking ''if one of those bullets ricochets, someone is going to get hurt.

Then, suddenly Tim Naylor fell backwards off his box, two of the others grabbing him. In a few minutes they were leading him to the boarding house, one eye completely shattered and hanging down his cheek. It was a sickening sight! Section-men rushed him to the junction on a speeder. We were told they had great difficulty in keeping him in hospital for even a day.

"I ain't going to miss it, anyway!" he declared. "What's the odds, when a fellow don't read."

One day in winter, when his camps were in full swing, Tim wanted to get to town in a hurry and borrowed a team of broncho ponies and cutter. Returning two days later, he bet some friends he could beat the train, leaving town at the same time. He did, crossing the tracks at Silver Mountain minutes ahead of the engine. Muffled in coonskin coat and cap, he stepped on the platform, exclaiming:

"It's the bronchos, not me, that wins the best! Why, we weren't many miles out of town when the wind started my eyes watering. First thing I knew, this blamed glass eye froze up. Then the good one froze, too! So I just give 'em their heads and here we are!".

Yes, he was a tough guy and no mistake, yet one of the kindest hearted, despite that stubborn streak where the rearing of his children were concerned. In all the twelve years of our acquaintenance and I knew him to be a heavy drinker at times, I never saw him ''the worse'', nor heard him use objectionable language when women were present.

CHAPTER FOUR

Headed For The Boundary

Owing to the closure of mines and big lumber camps, the Railway decided not to replace our agent; also to cut our train service to semi-weekly. It seemed crazy for me to be working and living under such unsatisfactory conditions when that station, containing six rooms, plus office and waiting-room, stood idle!

So I concocted a reciprocal agreement and submitted it to the regional Superintendent of the line. Pointing out that the building had already been broken into for the purpose of using the Company's phone, I suggested that in return for occupancy and fuel for heating I would act as caretaker, deliver train-orders, receive and send wires through their nearest despatcher. I would also hold myself responsible for way-freight left in the station shed. It was possibly an unusual offer from a lone woman, but I felt capable of handling things and needed a more permanent roof over my head.

Being already aware of the complicated machinery where railway companies' decisions are concerned, I sat back, fully prepared for at least two months to elapse before receiving a reply. It was, therefore, something of a shock when an O.C.S. (On Company's Service) letter was ceremoniously handed to me by next train, telling me to move in at once. Two Yale keys were enclosed.

Incidentally, the locks themselves had already been removed from the doors, a fact I had not mentioned when writing. Suspicions worked in the back of my mind! When

the ten-year-old son of a not-far distant neighbour came
over to watch preparations for moving in, I said:

"What do you know, Sammy? Someone has snitched
the locks from both my doors and I don't think it's going to
be very nice, living here without them. I have the keys, but
they're not a bit of use without locks. Neither are the locks
any use without keys so they've probably been thrown
away. You hunt around and see if you can find them. I'll
give you 25c for each."

He was back in five minutes, with both. I never did
fathom why the front door ws equipped with a cumbersome
latch (as might be seen on a barn door) instead of a door-
knob. It looked most incongruous beneath a Yale lock!

Before moving on, I had the living room fitted up as
a store, shelves completely covering two walls, a counter,
and a desk – all homemade and by volunteer labor [labour].
Some furniture, left in storage in Hamilton, was shipped
out for living quarters.

After being at the mines, where nothing was locked at
night except my bedroom door, it felt a bit odd to go around
checking five doors at the station, including freight-shed.
Before leaving Silver Mountain, Big Boss had given me a
revolver, saying it would be protection even if I were not
nervous living there alone. Many strangers (loggers) passed
through, to and from Pigeon River Camps, but in all the
years I was there, there was never any attempt to rob. There
chanced to be a stove-pipe hole in the floor of my bedroom,
immediately over the till – a good vantage point!

Well, here I was, modestly established in business and
finding it much to my liking, despite numerous vicissitudes.
Soon the existing Postmaster asked me if I would like to
take over his duties. He and his elder son spent much of
their time working in the woods; trains, very erratic as to
time of arrival, had to be met and mail bags carried to their

home. I was living at the station and ''tied'' by my business anyway, so postal duties would pose no problem. I made application to the authorities and was appointed. There wasn't much in it financially, salary being half the value of stamps sold, plus $15 quarterly for carrying mailbats. And I myself used as many stamps as were sold!

The former ticket office was ideal for the purpose, with wicket for handing out mail. In this part of the world butter came in bulk. It was cheaper and customers preferred buying that way. Wooden boxes, very well made and lined with wax paper, held 50 lbs. of butter. By using the lids to form partitions, these boxes served as excellent cubicles, ranged at each side of the wicket, with another tier above. Names, of course, were shown on each. There happened at the time to be a superabundance of Smiths calling for mail – 3 Charles and 5 Georges – some permanent, some transiet, and the only way to overcome the problem was to dub them Geo. 1, Geo. II and so on. But our reigning monarch being Geo. V, I had to use the last one's nickname, ''Sawdust'' Smith.

It took some little time to assess the types and trustworthiness of my customers, many of foreign birth, others native-born, but illiterate. In general, I would say the Finns were decidedly the best settlers, constructing first-class log buildings and largely able to live on the products of their land. On the other hand, many others took up Free Grant homesteads purely for the value of timber thereon and, when that was all gone, just left the district. Meantime, when a contract had put them on easy street for the time being, they squandered the proceeds and then turned to me for credit. Not all, of course, were of this type; but I soon found that unless I limited ''charge'' accounts, I might soon have been out of business! Then would come offers of cordwood or pulpwood, already cut on their land, half to be applied on the account and the balance for more groceries. Some of these folk owned no horses, which necessitated my buying a heavy team and hiring a teamster. He was a Finn and entirely satisfactory in every respect. After work one day, about three months later, he came to me and said: "Me like three days off; go town; get drunk."

A somewhat startling announcement, but I managed to keep a straight face while responding, ''That's O.K., Einar. I wouldn't want you to get drunk on the job.''. He was gone three days.

Keeping the team fully occupied meant buying standing timber and employing cutters. Thus was I gradually drawn into this phase of business – and before I really knew the difference between pine and spruce. Strange how one thing leads to another. As the Yorkshireman has it, "If it isn't summat, it's summat else!".

Looking back, I feel that my success in obtaining contracts with city dealers was a meticulous attention to specifications; for instance, piling would be in different lengths, varying from 35 to 75 feet, and must have a minimum top and maximum but diameter – according to length. It took an expert woodsman to judge these measurements in a standing tree, and it was wasteful to cut otherwise.

Life in the station-house was not all joy, though it was admittedly, at the time, a haven. The fuel provided was, of course, steam coal, mine-run – powerful but not too easy for a woman to handle, being either slack or huge lumps. The building, two-and-a-half feet above ground level, was sheeted but not banked. In the severe weather even with three stoves going everything on or near the floor would freeze. My only water supply was from the engine, the train-crew filling up a huge wooden barrel – originally used for coal-oil – whenever they had time. In summer, this stood on the platform, protected by a double cheese-cloth cover; in winter, in the waiting room. On specially cold nights, I'd wrap eggs and ink-bottles in an eiderdown quilt.

During seven years' occupancy, many interesting and some exciting things happened. One of the weirdest was being requested to give a night's shelter to the corpse of a drowned man. As there was no suitable material at the camp from which to make a rough-box, the remains were merely wrapped in canvas. The boarding-house had refused; and they were afraid of rats in the barn. I didn't know how long the poor fellow had been immersed, but thought of his relatives and said, "Yes."

One particular event of that first year stands out. The Pigeon River forms the International Boundary between N.W. Ontario and Minnesota, and large tracts of timber along its shore were being cut by one of the more important operators at the Lakehead. In the spring, logs would be driven downstream to Lake Superior, thence rafted to sawmills, Supplies, of course, had to come by rail, and for a number of years toting was done from my station, a distance of about 20 miles. Now, however, their camps had moved west and their freighting point was ten miles farther up the line.

One winter's afternoon, the phone rang and a voice said, ''This is the clerk from Camp Seven. Please send a wire to our city office and say that three of our men quit, and on their way to the track they were attacked. Two of them were murdered and the third badly beaten up managed to crawl back to camp. All were robbed of their time cheques.''

He then proceeded to give me the numbers of these, so that payment might be stopped. Well, it was pretty lengthy for a wire. Phoning would be quicker, anyway, so I got in touch with the agent at Stanley Junction, asking him to relay the message, immediately by municipal phone to the lumber company.

About 7 p.m. came a call from Sgt Simpson of the Provincial Police, saying he was proceeding by hand-car from Stanley Junction, a distance of twenty miles. "We'll try to reach Silver Mountain by ten," he said, "but please wait up for us, in case you have further news."

"O.K." I replied. "Meantime I'll phone the section-men west of here and as [ask] if any 'suspicious' persons have been seen around."

Prior to the First World War, gasoline "hand-cars" were unknown, in our district anyway. Hand-cars had to be pumped by hand. And the twenty miles were nearly all up grade!

Ten o'clock came, and no sign of them. Eleven o'clock, ditto. It had been a hard day and I was dog-tired. Yet I knew that were I to fall asleep upstairs, I'd never hear anyone at the door. So I carried a pillow, blanket and my loaded revolver down to the waiting-room and settled – more lress comfortabely – on one of the benches. Perhaps because there was a pleasant unaccustomed warmth from the big ugly stove (my bedroom being decidedly chilly). I dozed off in no time.

I heard neither the rumble of the hand-car nor the tramp of four men crossing the platform. What awakened me was the rattling of that huge door-latch! Besides Sgt. Simpson, there was a powerful Scandinavian, in the garb of a lumberjack but to my eyes, every inch a policeman, my friend Ted Naylor and a newspaper reporter. Hand-car trouble had delayed them and by this time it was 2 a.m.

As they filed in, looking cold and sorry for themselves, the Sergeant, spotting my paraphernalia on the bench, exclaimed:

"Don't tell me you've been sleeping here, in full view

of that window, with a murderer around!"

"And don't tell me," I countered, "that any murderer is deliberately walking right into your arms! It's much more on the books that he's heading in the opposite directon – towards the boundasry – at Gunflint Lake."

After warming up at the stove, the quartet departed to investigate any barns and buildings in the immediate neighbourhod, while I made coffee and toast and fried a plentiful supply of bacon. Finally – it must have been after 3.30 – they all trouped off to the boarding-house, front door of which was never locked. Any guests who chanced to arrive after the family had retired helped themselves to the first vacant room they found.

Then, having stoked up once more, I thankfully retired to my room. But not to bed – yet! There was a knock at the front door. Down I went. It was the burly Olsen and the news reporter, announcing that ''Tim wouldn't hear of a lady being left alone until they'd rounded up that murderer." They would sleep in the waiting-room. I could have offered them a bedroom, but somehow felt I'd helped ''the cause'' sufficiently for one night. At breakfast time, I learned that three of them had set off, by swift team for Camp Seven, short-cutting across Whitefish Lake; Olsen remained behind.

About ten o'clock, after hanging around the station, he said, "I think I'll take a stroll up the track."

Shortly after, a phone call came from North Lake, almost at end-of-steel, saying that the previous evening a man wearing skis [skiis} had been trying to buy .38 calibre cartridges. Just as I had thought – heading for the boundary!

The next thing I knew, Olsen was ushering two woodsmen into the waiting room. After locking the door, he began searching them. Meantime I was busy in the Post

Office preparing the mail for despatch. Olsen kept handing articles through the wicket to me; various items, including cartons of cigarettes, some silverware bearing hotel names and no fewer than three revolvers. Wrong again, thought I, not heading for the boundary!

The men could speak very little English. One kept saying, ''What for you want?'' and Olsen's reply was always the same, "You'll know – when you get to the police station!"

It transpired, however, that neither had any connection with the case in hand, though they were wanted for petty thievery. Olsen's stroll up the tracks had not been entirely fruitless.

When the Sergeant and his companions returned from Camp Seven, we learned there had been no actual murder. The two men, thought by the third to be dead, were so badly beaten up as to require hospital treatment.

No trace of the brutal attacker was ever found. Neither were the time cheques presented for payment. After all, trying to cash them would have been a dead giveaway. Thinking he had, intentionally or otherwise, committed murder, his safest bet was to feel the country.

Yes, it was generally conceded that my original assumption was correct – he had headed fo rthe boundary.

CHAPTER FIVE

Adventure in Cordwood

Few people would associate excitement, intrigue, adventure – yes, even tragedy! -- with so plebian a commodity as cordwood. In pioneering, particularly, ''venture'' has a habit of transforming itself into ''adventure''.

Dealing with varied types of people and unexpected happenings tends to sharpen one's faculties, often demanding instant decisions.

The train had pulled in only a few minutes before and as I busily sorted the mail, a big swarthy stranger came over to the wicket.

"I want to see Mr. Mitchell!" he boomed at me.

"There is no Mr. Mitchell," I mildly rejoined. And, before I could explain further, he interrupted, "Then I want to see the boss!"

By this time, his manner was becoming irksome, particularly since he must have seen I was busy, so, staring him straight in the eye, I announced firmly, "I am the boss."

This announcement seemed to take the wind out of his sails, as, turning away, he grunted, "Don't do business with woman."

"Your privilege!" I shot after the retreating figure.

One evening, shortly after this little encounter, the phone rang. It was Rex Tibbetts, my nearest fellow-Post-Master-storekeeper, 5 1/2 miles down the line, saying:

"How's chances to pick up a couple of cars of cordwood in your neighbourhood? I've contracted to ship a train-load to Winnipeg and am two cars short."

"I don't know," I answered, "I'm not interested in

it myself, except occasionally in trade. Can't you get it around Nolalu? Every time I pass, there are acres of the stuff piled at the siding."

"That's true. But practically all our settlers are Finns, and they trade with their own Co-Op. I've arranged with the railway company to have cars spotted at any point necessary, and it will be on a Sunday, probably two weeks from tomorrow."

Roads were not good enough for truck or tractor, and summer-hauling, by wagon, was scarcely profitable. However, with cars placed near the source of supply, I experienced no difficulty in filling my neighbour's need.

The general procedure for a ''special'' of this kind was for the caboose to be coupled to the engine, with the required number of boxcars bringing up the rear. This enabled the crew to drop them off at specified points on the track, spending a few hours – probably fishing – near the ''Y'' on which the engine was reversed; then pick up the loaded cars. It was the custom, on reaching the next siding, to switch so that the engine was ahead.

On the appointed Sunday the train passed through in mid-morning and returned about two o'clock. Rex, who was aboard, and the conductor came in (the latter to 'phone the despatcher) and I gained the impression they'd had a drink or two. Could that fact account for their not bothering to switch, leaving the station with two cars ahead of the engine? Within the next few miles they would have to traverse a winding, steep down-grade. Awkward for the engineer, one would imagine?

Just recently I'd helped the section foreman, who was an Austrian, write an exam. Perhaps it would be more accurate to say I helped him study the handbooks and wrote the exam for him. By the time we were through, I probably knew more about Railway Rules and Regulations than he did! At any rate, a few minutes after the ''special'' left, the sequence of blasts from the engine-whistle told me the warning was ''Danger – Keep clear of the track.''

Later that evening Rex phoned to tell me that those two loaded cars ahead of the engine had broken away and careened down the grade, gaining such momentum it was impossible to catch up with them. Then the inevitable happened. The runaways crashed in to the first loaded car they reached. Unfortunately, it was not quite loaded and the owner of the wood was inside. He was killed instantly, crushed beyond recognition as a human being. "Just jelly!" one of the rescuers described the remains.

This tragedy effectually put an end to the practice of loading cars on the main track.

As previously stated, I was not personally interested in cordwood, except as trade and barter. Some settler who lacked cash might say, "I need hay and oats. Will you take cordwood (or ties) in trade?" Another would say, "Could you sell a car of dry birch for me?" Many being of foreigh birth – Finnish, German, Austrian, Dutch, Polish – they could not write in English, and the deal would have necessitated a trip to the city.

On one such occasion, I shipped a load of first class dry wood billed in my own name, of course, to Mansons's, one of the most reputable dealers in the district. Cheque in settlement was so long delayed, I paid Hyyryla, a man with a big family, then penned a polite request that the company oblige by paying me. They had the nerve to deny ever having received the shipment; and persisted in their assertion. That made me mad! I immediately wrote to the Railway's department in Winnipeg where I knew record was kept of all car movements, asking that they trace boxcar No. 71896 from the time it left my station on a certain date, naming the consignee. A prompt reply showed that it had been delivered to Manson's on the following day, and picked up from their yard, empty, two days later. So I entered suit in Division Court. Having such tangible evidence of my claim, it didn't seem necessary to engage a lawyer. Manson's merely notified the court that their foreman, who should have given evidence, was off duty with a broken arm; they were not represented. The Magistrate awarded me not only the amount owing, but interest for six months and my expenses.

This should have been a warning to leave cordwood alone, but it didn't seem to have that effect. Some months later, when a letter arrived from the Klondyke Fuel Dealers, Winnipeg, asking if I could ship them a train-load, and naming a very fair price, I said to myself, "Ah, ha! My fame is spreading!" Naturally, I replied that a train-load was out of the question, but I could ship three cars, at intervals, if that would suit them. This method of shipment proved agreeable.

Over a period of several months, there came courteous letters, appreciative of the quality of the wood and enclosing cheques of from $150 to $200 ''on account''; never specific payments for individual shipments. When the agreed number of cars had been delivered, their cheque in final settlement was $130 short of the correct sum. I returned the cheque, protesting the discrepancy. In response, they claimed that every load had been measured by the City Fuel Inspector, so they couldn't be wrong in their measure.

Making inquiries, I discovered that other unsuspecting folk on this branch line had been gypped in the same manner but had done nothing about it. "Winnipeg is so far away," they said, "a thirteen-hour journey after one got to the Lakehead, and would cost more than the shortage." Well, I wanted to get to the bottom of it, so, armed with all my bills-of-lading, I headed for the city and thence to the Manitoba capital.

Next morning, early, I hunted up the fuel inspector in the railway yards, and found him most friendly. Checking records with my car numbers, he announced that only two of the early ones had been certified by him. "I'm real glad that someone is at last getting after that darn crooked outfit! They been running this game too long. And if you have to take them to Court, lady, I'll be tickled to death to appear as a witness."

I thanked him but said I hoped to settle the manner personally, with the dealer, now that I had this evidence. That was my next "port of call" – a modest little office on a modest side street. A polite young man was in attendance, who claimed ignorance of the whole deal. He said his Dad looked after finances. Could I call in the afternoon? On my arrival at 3 p.m. another young man was on duty; he was extremely sorry, but Dad had been called out of town. Could I call tomorrow?

This appeared rather deliberate, and I wasn't prepared to play hide-and-seek indefinitely. Perhaps a little strategy might work! Ascertaining the dealer's home address, through the obliging fuel inspector, I paid a surprise visit in the early evening. There was no response to my several rings, though movements within were clearly audible. Taking a walk around the block, I passed again, on the opposite side of the street. And whom should I espy, emerging from a side door, but my swarthy acquaintenace – ''Don't do business with woman''! – at which my fighting ancestors arose within me. The decision was made.

Next morning, the hotel desk clerk recommended a very reliable lawyer, a Mr. Downing. I put everything in his hands and boarded the next train home.

It took fully three months to collect the amount due.

Then the lawyer sent me a cheque for the full $130, saying he had been so much interested in the case, and its probable effect in protecting others, I was to pay him just what I felt I could spare.

On the whole, I quite enjoyed my first visit to the Manitoba metropolis, though the incident leading up to it had dampened my ardour for cordwood. Somehow I felt, too, that Klondyke Fuel Dealers would have even less desire, in the future, to "do business with woman".

CHAPTER SIx

Paddy Reappears

Nothing had been heard of Paddy O'Connor since he was carried from the Mines in an apparently crippled condition.

Then one day he hopped off the train, looking very spry and bringing with him a young woman of foreign extraction whom he introduced as ''the missus''. She spoke few words of English, he none of her language, but they looked supremely happy. In addition to a wife, Paddy had acquired a Free Grant Homestead, 160 acres, 3 1/2 miles "out", smilingly taking it for granted the neighbours would help build a log house thereon. As a matter of record, they did all the work, while he stood around keeping them in good humour by witty sayings.

As years passed and the O'Connor family increased, inevitably the time came when credit was needed. Sometimes a small portion of the bill was paid. Then the indebtedness increased until it became necessary to call a halt.

"To be sure!" said Paddy, "and I'll be seein' yer p'int. I've a ton and a half of good hay I'll be after givin' ye." On the strength of which promise, credit was again extended.

When I sent a team out to haul the hay, Paddy had just traded it for a cow! His only explanation – ''Sure and me nippers had to be fed milk.'' Which seemed reasonable enough. What could one do?

One day, in the winter of 1916, I was travelling to the city when Paddy seated himself beside me and without preamble said, "I'll be hearin' they need men pretty bad, and I'm on me way to jine up."

A week or so later, after a three-foot snowfall, a young
Finnish neighbour of the O'Connors came out on skis to
catch the train. He asked if Paddy had made arrangements
with me to supply his family; that Mrs. O'Connor had
nothing but milk from the cow and a sack of flour – and the
baby only three weeks old. On his return, he would be glad
to carry a few items to her, but not weighing more than ten
pounds, skiing being very difficult on the soft snow.

After gathering a few essentials, I scurried around
among the near neighbours, trying to find a man who would
go out that day. Each one said it would be impossible to
wade all that distance through such deep snow, for the last
two miles, at least, the road had not been broken all winter.

At that time, there were only two trains per week, and
I just had to report to the authorities in town next day.
Directly after lunch, I started out, wearing snowshoes.
Now, unless you've tried them on a ski-trail, you've no
idea of the effort involved. Every now and then – my
footwear being three times the width of the ski – one foot
would slide off sideways into the soft, deep snow. And
not so much as a twig to hang onto, while recovering
that extremity and its clumsy appendage! Although the
temperature was below zero, I was so hot from the exertion,
parka and coat were flying open. Half way there, I paused,
wondering, "Can I make it?". Then, deciding the return trip
would be easier on a "broken" trail, I continued.

Finally the house sitting in the middle of a vast white
space, loomed into sight, its high-pitched roof giving it
the look of a barn. As I drew near, three little faces peered
through the front window and at sound of my knock, six
little feet scurried away. By the time their Mother admitted
me, they were all hiding behind the cook-stove. The
home was little more than a shelter – just one huge space,
possibly 25x35 feet, without partitions or ceiling. The floor

was dirt and very uneven with the exception of one corner where a floor of hewed logs accommodated table and benches. In other corners were two-tier bunks. In the centre sat a woefully inadequate box-stove, a mere pretense at heating such space.

Mrs. O'Connor welcomed me heartily, but as though I were merely making an afternoon call, mentioning nothing of her predicament until directly questioned. Knowing, now, that Paddy was in the armed forces, I suggested it would be better that the family move to town, to which she agreed. Meantime, the children, who had probably never seen a woman, other than their mother, crept out from their hideaway and forgot their fear when cookies and candy emerged from my little packsack.

The Patriotic League in Port Arthur, notified of the situation, offered to find suitable accommodation and asked me to have the whole family come down as soon as possible. I despatched two of my heaviest teams to bring them out to the station. Breast-high in snow, the horses had to push their way through, the teams taking turn about.

I wish I had a picture of the outfit as it loomed in sight – four tired horses, and aboard the sleigh the mother, four children, a big trunk and a calf, the cow hoofing it behind.

In due course, Paddy was drafted overseas. On board ship, cutting up to entertain his comrades, again he tied himself in knots. He spent two years in British hospitals and convalescent homes. Men of the same battalion said he never set foot in France, which was ridiculous. Even a "silvery tongue" could hardly have achieved the comfortable pension with which Paddy was discharged! Not only this, but he obtained the limit of Veteran-homesteader grant from the Canadian Government, returning to Silver Mountain covered with glory and accompanied by a boxcar containing a fine team of horses, feed, implements, seed and groceries.

But Paddy never had been and never would be a farmer. He couldn't handle the team as well as young Tommy, then nine years old. Eventually the O'Connors decided homesteading was no good, and, anyway, they could live on his pension in town.

The homestead, horses and implements were returned to a kindly Government and the family moved away for keeps. I lost sight of them completely.

Many years later, while living in Port Arthur, I took my luncheon daily at the same cafe. My usual waitress, a very quiet girl, stood hesitantly beside my table one day and said, shyly, "Could you be the Miss Mitchell who used to live at Silver Mountain?"

"Why, yes!" I replied. "Whose little girl were you?"

"I was the Paddy O'Connor baby, three weeks old when you had us all brought out through the snow. My parents often speak of you."

CHAPTER SEVEN

Contract With Queer Angles

The time arrived when I didn't have to seek contracts. Queries came from firms in the cities, asking if I could supply certain materials.

Just before World War I, a number of grain elevators were to be built in Port Arthur and Fort William. This meant an unusual demand for piles. To the uninitiated, I might explain that a "pile" is a tree, stripped of limbs (usually pine or spruce) and of varied lengths. These are driven into the lake-bed by powerful machines – "cheek by jowl" – to form a foundation for enormous concrete elevators, the largest I remember being capable of storing 7 million bushels of wheat.

The first really imposing contract offered me was for 3000 or more pieces of piling in lengths of from 35 to 75 feet, with specified top and butt diameter. This involved finding sub-contractors among the settlers who had suitable timber.

I'd had satisfactory dealings with these people before, and it struck me as odd that my appointment for finalizing the contract should be in the evening. It didn't take long to realize why! Seated in the Company's office, and doing most of the talking, was the manager of another business house (not timber); quite obviously a "silent partner" in the firm and helping finance it.

Carefully reading the contract, I handed it back, saying, "No, I can't sign that!" All three looked astonished.

"Why not?" asked the Boss. "Aren't we offering a fair

price?"

"The price is O.K. But the contract reads 'to be inspected at point of delivery'. I want it inspected when loaded."

This bruoght loud protestations; all their contracts read that way.

"If that's defnite, I don't want one," I said. "You undertake to pay 50 percent when material is piled at the track, balance on delivery. But remember, I'll be buying from the settlers in the district, which means they will require at least 70 precent in wages, groceries and horse-feed. So the culling must be done on the spot. Otherwise, how shall I know from which of these sub-contracts the culled stuff comes?"

This was a reasonable contention, and since they needed the material pretty badly, wording was changed to suit me.

All this happened fifty years ago, and I still have a complete record of the transaction. I sold over 3000 piles, with a total footage of 114,300 feet and value of $7,530. It was an imposing sight, "decked" 10 feet high alongside the railway siding about seven miles up the line, awaiting instructions for delivery.

Another "angle" in connection with this particular undertaking caused a certain amount of annoyance. Two Finns formed a partnership and secured a sub-contractor from me. Besides groceries, they required a horse, hay and oats; so by the time their piling was delivered at the track they had received about 80 percent. Then, although much of it was not yet shipped, I paid Suomi and Nikkala the balance. A few weeks later, much to my surprise, I received a lawyer's letter, saying that Suomi contended that he had not received what was due to him. Calling on this man-of-law when next in the city, it was revealed that Nikkala had more than his share, because he had the horse! This was ridiculous , of course, everything having been charged to the partnership. How could I know who eventually got the horse? The lawyer was disgusted and said he would have nothing to do with the case. "On the contrary, I want you to take it to Court. I'm getting tired of Suomi's crazy accusations every time he returns from the city, half intoxicted!". Naturally I won the case.

Unfortunately, when a fair portion of my contract had duly been shipped to the elevators, the demand for piling ceased. War was in the air, and construction stopped. This is doubtless what sparked insurance against fire on the remainder; followed, in due course, by a gigantic conflagration! I went up on the train and we sped past at unusual speed, flames licked the coach windows. Later, several empty 5-gallon gasoline cans were discovered, thrown away in nearby bush. The agent who placed the insurance did not get 14 years in jail as did an Adjustor recently in the news. He skipped town and was never traced. After this, the Boss-Manager evaded paying the balance of the indebtedness, saying that destruction by fire did not constitute delivery! I counted myself lucky to lose only $450 on the deal.

On account of continued business depression, many of the larger timber companies closed their camps. In most cases, it had been the custom to keep a few farm animals – cows, pigs and poultry – which were, of course, sold when discharging the employees. Among the latter, a very fine elderly man, a Pole known as "Daubrey", had been in sole charge of the "barnyard" at a timber camp in my area for several years. Being able to get all he needed in the way of clothing and tobacco from the camp "van", he invariably arranged to have his wages, less deductions, deposited to his bank account.

The depression increased; many could not find employment. Then, one day in the following summer, Daubrey presented himself at my place. I believe he had tramped the 40 miles from town. "Please you give me job? – board , no pay." I really had no work for him, but couldn't refuse the poor fellow and set him to clear land. After a couple of weeks, he approached me with a modest request. "Please you let me have two dollar? I send to my wife."

"Of course! But is that enough?"

Then, in faltering English, the whole story came out. When the camps finally closed down, he had gone to the bank to draw some of his savings. The teller told him, "You must see the Manager." And, to use Daubrey's own words – "I go in office to see him. He sit with gun on the desk, and say 'No! You get no money. You enemy alien!'"

Russia, although not at war with Poland, had overrun that country at the beginning of World War I, had stolen cattle and other possessions before burning the homes of small farmers. His wife and family had since been living in a hole in the ground. Because they were near the border, and he knew an honest Russian peddlar who travelled the district with his wares, it had been possible for Daubrey to occasionally send money to his wife. Now, with conditions so much worse, he wasn't sure if this fellow could get across. Hence, the very small sum he asked for.

Not long afterwards, Daubrey secured a good job and was able to send to Poland for his family; but I never heard if he finally "retrieved" his savings.

Happily, though, there were contracts without queer angles. A construction firm in the city required white-pine square timbers measuring 8x10 inches and in various lengths, for building a new breakwater in Port Arthur's harbour. For this I was able to purchase the cutting rights on a Government Timber Limit a few miles away, in

Fraleigh Township. It necessitated putting in a camp of from 20 to 30 men, extra teams, employing a foreman and hiring a portable sawmill. There was an extraordinarily good cut of white pine, most of it sound to the roots (quite unusual) and so big that four of these 8x10's could be cut from even the second log.

This contract did not materialize until rather late in the logging season, and snow was beginning to melt before everything was hauled to the track. For a while, it was necessary to sprinkle roads with water late at night, using a homemade water cart or sleigh then haul very early next morning while frozen.

When this and later winter camps were in operation, I was fortunate in having Pierre, a French Canadian, as foreman for a long time. Not only was he thoroughly versed in all phases of the lumbering industry, but was well-liked by the men under his control. Leo, the cook, and Harold, the barn-boss, came back year after year. They had no home ties and usually let most of their earnings accumulate until spring "break up".

Shortly after one of these closures of camp, I was in the city, talking to someone, when Leo came across the street and asked rather sheepishly if I could lend him two dollars. Naturally I thought it a joke, and passed it off as such. My companion said, "Oh, he's probably broke. There's always a gang of their friends waiting at the railway station for guys coming out from camp this time of the year. First they get them drunk, then 'roll them'." It seemed fantastic! To work hard all winter, then be robbed of six or seven hundred dollars!

Harold, I later learned, would sometimes get no farther than the Stanley Junction hostelry, only half way to the city. It seemed that one drink would finish him.

Such happenings led me to make inquiries through

discreet quarters about these two men, as a result of which I felt it my duty to more-or-less "mother" them. Neither resented it. Indeed, when Leo came to work the following fall, he told me he had an old father, living alone and on the Old Age Pension (then about $20) and that on account of having been robbed last spring, he'd been unable to give him anything. I said, "Leo, why not authorize me to send him something, even a small amount, every month out of your pay?" He agreed heartily.

Harold's nearest relative was a sister, Superintendent of a Hospital in Montreal. Finally he too confided in me; for the past two years he had promised to visit her in the spring, but his money "went". A very simple solution to this was for me to buy him a return ticket to Montreal, with his consent, and deduct the amount from wages due. That time he really made – and thoroughly enjoyed – the trip!

It was a curious experience, looking after the affairs of people so much older than myself, but very rewarding.

During the earlier years of my timber activities, I had sold railroad ties to a man in the city, in common with all the settlers on this branch line who would assuredly thus earn a fairly good commission for the service. After a while, I found that most of my neighbours within a radius of several miles preferred to sell to me, chiefly because they could get all they needed in the way of supplies, feed and so on, without the necessity of going to the city.

One day, alighting from the train at Port Arthur, I ran into this "buyer", and said "Would you have any objection to my obtaining a tie contract direct with the C.N.R.?"

"Certainly not," was his response.

I took the night train to Winnipeg, and next morning had an interview with the Company's purchasing agent. After hearing my errand, he said: "I admire your ambition to have a contract direct with us and would be glad to award you one. On the other hand, we already have an understanding, not an actual contract, with this man buying for us. I therefore feel it necessary to first obtain his consent, by wiring. Come to my offce at 10 tomorrow morning."

As I entered at the appointed time, the gentleman looked annoyed, then handed me the reply. "Certainly object to Miss Mitchell having contract."

"I'm extremely sorry about this," said the courteous official, "and I'll certainly have something to say to that man the next time I see him! Meantime, I hope you asked for a pass to come to Winnipeg."

"No, I never thought of it as Company business."

And back I went to Port Arthur and home.

I don't remember how many thousand ties I already had, piled beside the track representing idle money, of course. The next time Mr. x showed up at Silver Mountain, he said, "Well, Miss Mitchell, when are you going to sell me your ties?"

"I'm not!" I smilingly rejoined. I always refrained from showing the least annoyance when people played mean tricks; it kept them wondering.

The same query came on subsequent occasions. On one, I said, "I may sell to the C.P.R. The two companies are co-operative, you know." On another, "Maybe I'll just insure them."

Finally, when time was running out, and his contract not filled, he offered a substantially higher price. I accepted it.

Years later, one of his daughters told me, with a tinge of amusement, she'd heard her father say to a business associate, "You have to be up before breakfast to get the better of Miss Mitchell!"

Maybe I'd taught him a lesson. I hope so.

CHAPTER EIGHT

I Buy Timber

As Friday's biweekly local puffed into our station, I stood, in drenching rain, to receive the mail-bags, usually thrown to or at me (I was never sure which) but this time the baggage-master hopped off, carrying them over his arm and motioned me towards the waiting-room. Here he dived into the numerous pockets of his blue jeans, finally locating a crumpled scrap of paper.

"For you," he remarked. Then, under his breath, "And Pierre says to do it pronto! There's an outfit in town sending a man up on the next train after it."

On the bit of paper were scribbled just three words BUY ZANIC'S TIMBER. I knew what they meant. Pierre, my very efficient foreman, was in the city endeavouring to increase an existing contract for piling, provided the necessary standing timber was procurable. Hauling any distance during spring break-up was out of the question. Zanic's property ran alongside the track, and having previously sized things up, I knew exactly what to offer.

But it wasn't as simple a matter as those three little words implied. How was I to get there? The very primitive wagon-road, as a result of copious rainfall, combined with melting snow, was impassable. The railway-track was the only answer, and I certainly had no intention of "hoffing it" the eight miles each way, in that weather!

These pros and cons chased through my mind while sorting the meagre mail. Instead of feeling flattered that Pierre considered me, a mere woman, capable of tackling an awkward situation, I was rather annoyed that he had not returned to do it himself.

At Whitefish Lake, four miles beyond my place, a big timber-contractor, having insufficient barn-space for idle teams, had the surplus stabled near our station. Yes, I'm harking back to the days when men were men and horses were not tractors! I rang up the clerk and said, "How's chances to borrow a saddle with a horse attached – tomorrow?"

"Good!" was the reply. "I'll have Terry go down early afternoon and pick you one."

Terry was the barn-boss, an ex-cowboy from N.W. States, and in his early forties. I liked the way in which he talked to his charges as he passed my place each day, herding them down to water at the creek. That was all I knew of him.

Not having a saddle horse of my own, indeed, not having ridden for years I possessed no suitable togs, but made do with a pair of corduroy pants from stock, high boots and a heavy wool coat. A slicker would have been more protective! Thus garbed, with pen, paper and $100 tucked in an inside pocket, I answered Terry's knock at 2 p.m. next day. He had tethered the two horses to opposite ends of a flat-car on the siding. As I opened the door, each was lashing out with one hind hoof in an effort to kick the other.

"They're a bit fresh, ma'am, I reckon," came in a Western drawl. "Not been out o' the born, 'cept to water, for couple o' weeks."

We rode away, following the narrow foot-trail alongside the track. Before reaching Whitefish Lake, my mount cast a shoe, which had to be replaced by the camp blacksmith. Naturally I had intended to continue my trip alone, but when Terry offered to come along, I said, "Sure, I'll be glad of your company. I may even be asking you to witness an agreement." Privately, I thought he was not too sure I could handle the distinctly nervous animal assigned to me.

It was anything but a joy-ride! Rain persisted in a

relentless manner and as we were travelling 'Indian file', conservation was next to impossible. Small culverts, constructed of poles, were unable to cope with overflow from streams swollen by melting snow, causing ponds to form on the upper side of the railway-track.

Looking and feeling like half-drowned rats, we arrived at the Zanic homestead, only to learn he was away, fishing. After outlining my offer to Mrs. Zanic, who was sure her husband would gladly accept, we sat around in soppy garments while she made tea. The wood stove smoked at every seam. Even the tea was flavoured with it! Or could we have been drinking kini-kinik, Indian tea, made from bark? At any rate, it was hot and comforting.

Promising to be back next day, we started on the return trip, Terry in the lead. Presently I heard the sudden crunch of rotten timbers as his horse broke through a culvert. Instantly he shouted to me, "Take the other side!"

Perhaps I wheeled my mount too quickly. Anyway, in the swift change of direction, one of his shoes became firmly wedged between two railway ties, throwing him to his knees. I got him up, but down he went again! On rising the second time, however, the hoof was free. He took one leap, landing in the middle of a fair-sized pond, scared stiff and trembling in every muscle. Not until I had piloted him back on to the rail, leaning forward to pat him on the neck, did I notice Terry. Rigid in the saddle, eyes and mouth agape, he blurted out, "Well, I'll be jiggered...thinking of the horse!"

"Certainly. Wouldn't you? The poor brute's as nervous as a kitten." From then on, the "poor brute" shied at every puddle.

Nearing the camp, I begged my escort to quit the cavalcade and let me lead his horse back to the barn; there seemed to be no sense in his accompanying me and then having to walk four miles back to camp. Eventually he agreed, on condition that he see me safely over a broken culvert that had to be jumped. "You see, ma'am, they mightn't take it together."

This little hazard passed, Terry slipped a halter over his mount's head, tying the lead-rope to the pummel of my saddle. It felt good to be nearing home again! Passing the Silver Mountain Hostel, I called to a young lad to ask his father to come over to the stable and feed the horses, happy that excitement was over for the day. Not so! While waiting at the barn, the spare horse decided that, before retiring, a roll was in order. Every time he rolled, my mount and I were jerked violently sideways until, much to my relief, the halter broke.

That evening, after supper, Terry phoned. "Say! I can borrow a speeder and take you up the line on Sunday if that'll suit? Section boss says there's a tie-train goin' west right early, but it'll be O.K. So long as we watch for her comin' back."

I gladly accepted. It would be quicker, even if less eventful. Sunday dawned a bright, clear day. Progress was not noticeably swift on the litttle three-wheel contraption, the road being mostly up-grade. When little more than half way to Zanic's homestead, we heard the engines whistle as the train approached. The line was single-track, so we lifted the speeder off and seated ourselves on the nearby rock.

Then came the shock of my thirty years. Without the least attempt at preliminaries, Terry suddenly grasped my left hand and blurted out – "How do you think we'd get along in double harness?"

I stared at him in bewilderment for a moment, but quickly sensed from the anxious, pleading expression in his dark eyes – that this was a genuine proposal of marriage. I was speechless! Mercifully the train came noisily around the bend and thundered past, giving me a few moments in which to collect my wits. Was the man crazy? Why, until yesterday, we had never even spoken to each other! Could it be because I'd 'stayed put' when my horse fell? All this flashed thorugh my mind while the train passed.

"I'm terribly sorry!" I then said. "But there is someone else – a long way from here." It was the only white lie that came to me, on the spur of the moment, that might save his feelings.

After this, neither had much to say while heading for our destination. There was merely a two-room shack, with a couple of tumble down out-buildings. As I stood waiting for the door to open, Terry murmered, "Reckon I'll go visit the pigs while you get your business talk."

Expecting a reasonably pleasant reception, I was surprised at Zanic's dour, almost guilty expression as he asked me in, his wife disappearing into the bedroom without a word. Ignoring these peculiar signs, I began, "Well, Mr. Zanic, your wife has no doubh told you of my offer for the spruce and pine on your property. How do you feel about it?"

With downcast eyes he pulled forward a chair for me, and hesitantly replied, "The missus, you see, she couldn't just mind what your offer was. Excited, I guess. And I wasn't sure as you'd be coming up again, so....well. ... when Bailey's man came up on the tie-train... I just signed up with him."

What a situation! My foreman had in all probability secured an extension of the piling contract on the strength of my buying this particular standing timber.

"I think, Mr. Zanic, you might at least have given me the first chance. However, it's your timber and naturally you can please yourself. Possibly, too, Mr. Bailey's offer is better than mine." At this point, he promplty produced the document for me to read, asking that I explain it to him.

"To begin with, it's an entirely different agreement from

mine. I wanted to buy the timber standing, my own men and
teams doing the work. You would have had $100 in cash
to bind the bargain, and the balance as soon as shipped.
According to the Bailey contract, YOU do all the cutting,
hauling and loading on cars. Apart from their $200 down,
you get no more until thirty days after delivery.”

“The dirty crook! He never told me that. I’ve no dough
to hire men and teams. Two hundred bucks ain’t no use!”

There was nothing further to be said, so I departed. Terry
joined me, saying “Reckoned you’d be calling me in to be
witness?”

“No, the deal’s off! Zanic has sold to Bailey’s men who
came up on that tie-train. Funny, isn’t it. He passed us, on his
way back to town, an hour ago.”

“Funny nothing!” was the explosive response, “and I
hope he gets gypped on the deal.”

“Actually,” I informed him, ‘’a contract signed on a
Sunday is illlegal, but I didn’t tell Zanic that. He showed
it to me; obviously he hadn’t read it itself. Not witnessed
either.”

I expected Pierre, when he returned on Tuesday’s train,
to be concerned at the bad news awaiting him. Before I
could say anything, however, he broke in , “Everything’s
hunky-dory! I saw Zanic in town today. He’d been to a
lawyer and had the Bailey deal quashed. It was signed on
Sunday and not even witnessed.”

“But what gave Zanic the idea it was illegal?? I did not
tell him..”

“Oh, he says Terry rode up to his place and put him wise.
I’m to tell you Zanic will be back on Friday, and to have the
contract ready for him to sign.”

So, after all, I did buy timber.

CHAPTER NINE

A Spinster Homesteads

With much more commodious premises and ample storage-space in the freight-shed, I had considerably increased my stock, including dry goods, men's footwear and overalls, drugs, even coal oi. At one stage, I dsiplayed razors, but finding they were often stolen, discontinued this line.

But no sooner was one problem solved than others would pop up. After all, my main object in coming to Canada had been to eventually have my mother and sister join me. Would they like living in the bush? How or where could I provide a suitable home? I would never consider the station-house as such; there was no cultivated land attached, no particular view and it was horribly difficult to heat in winter, not to mention the lack of home peacefulness, the store being open on weekdays until 8 p.m. All the nearby homesteads were "settled" and none for sale.

Then one day a resourceful neighbour said, "Why don't you make application to the Crown Lands Dept. for one of the discarded mining-claims in the vicinty? I know of several 80-acre ones that have reverted to the Crown for non-payment of taxes."

"Eighty acres!" I gasped. "What in Heaven's name would I do with all the land? I've certainly no desire to be a farmer."

"That's simple," said my adviser. "You can built on one corner of it – the nearest to the track – just clearing enough land to protect the buildings from bush-fires. Besides, you'll always be assured of fuel, which is 'something' in our climate."

After mulling the suggestion over, I decided it might be worth looking into on my next visit to the city.

"I'd like to apply for homestead rights on Lot R.140, Lybster Township," I announced.

His expression was almost pitying as, with some finality, he answered, "We don't grant free homesteads to unmarried women."

"But," I insisted, "I'm the head of the family. My mother is a widow and she has no sons. The business I am developing in the district warrants my having them join me, which means I must provide a suitable home."

Finding me hard to discourage, he eventually drew out a form, and, with an unmistakeable sneer on his countenance, his response came grudgingly.

"Oh, well, I'll take your application, but you may as well understand right now that it won't do you any good! Only recently, the Department has turned down two applications from widows!"

Obviously there was no hope of my desires being furthered in this quarter, so next day I wrote a long letter to the Minister of Lands and Forsets, Toronto, stating my case. It took two months – apparently requiring serious consideration by gentlemen in high places! – but then, to my great joy, the authorization came through, accompanied by an extremely nice letter from the Minister himself, congratulating me on being the first unmarried woman so honoured in Ontario. Years later, when in Toronto for a visit, I called on this gentleman. The first thing which met my eye in the outer lobby of the Parliament Bldgs., was a huge block of quartz, liberally sprinked with ore, from the West End Silver Mines at Silver Mountain. Its weight must have been nearly a ton!

And now to discover the boundary lines of my property. It seemed possible to get only a vague idea, since during the period of non-registered ownership these abandoned claims had become happy hunting grounds for timber-thieves. The original blazed trees, indicating the lines, had been deliberately removed. The lots were stripped of the best, and presented no appeal to a would-be settler, who usually depended on selling a certain amount of timber to finance development.

I learned from the Township map that Lot R.140 lay on both sides of the road leading from the station to the mines. About mid-way, close to the road, was a wonderful spring of the purest water, always ice-cold, seeping from the rocky mountainside; it never froze over, even in 40-below-zero weather. Beside it, someone had driven a short stake, on which hung a rusty old meat tin. This I dubbed "the loving cup", because everyone used it (not two at a time though; it was too small). I wonder what one would think if asked to drink from a communal unwashed cup in a hotel! Probably this tin's constant subjection to sun, pure air, rain and frost guaranteed its purity.

The man engaged to clear the initial two acres had lived in the district for a number of years, and claimed familiarity with all the lines. He insisted that the beautiful spring was on my lot, so I promptly decided that was the logical place to build (despite it being a good half-mile and mostly uphill from the railway), a supply of pure water being an absolute essential.

After the two acres had been cleared, and the man paid, it transpired that was not my land at all – merely adjoined it. I never found it convenient to employ him again.

Eventually I chose a far better location, only five minutes walk from my business, and almost on the other end of the lot, it being half a mile long by one quarter wide. Here, too, there was an excellent spring creek – also from the mountain.

In the case of such Free Grant lands, the Provincial Government naturally imposed certain conditions and requirements. Settlers must build a dwelling at least 16x20 feet and occupy it not less than six months out of every twelve. He (or she!) must clear and cultivate two acres of land per year in order to gain clearance from Crown dues when selling some types of timber – in this district, chiefly pine. Considerably increased cultivation must be done if the grantee desires full title to the land. In this connection, a case comes to mind where a man certainly "got away with murder". Purposely timing his application for deed in midwinter, he showed the Homestead Inspector a beautiful expanse of level, cleared land – and was granted title. We neighbours knew that most of this "clearing" was a small frozen-over lake, nicely camouflaged with three feet of snow, and wondered if the inspector had been fooled or bribed.

The building-site eventually selected was a plateau, in one direction sloping towards Beaver Creek (over which it was necessary to build a seventy-foot bridge), in another to an excellent spring rivulet and the third, well, just into the woods.

The hewed-log original structure measured 20x30 feet, and had a half-pitch roof. This gave an 18-foot square living-dining room combined and two smallish bedrooms; ample for a start, as there were three bedrooms at the station and I intended usually to sleep there myself. A fairly large amount of currency had to be kept on hand, since lumberjacks coming out from Company camps couldn't spend anything unless their time-cheques were cashed.

When buying materials, such as roofing, windows, etc. from a wholesale hardware dealer in the city, I mentioned a special-dimension window I wanted for my mother's bedroom. It was to be long and not too high, because I planned a wide sill, with little cupboards and drawers beneath.

The Manager's expression was doubting. "I don't think, Miss Mitchell, that such a size is made. However, I'll call up the sash factory." Apparently the response was negative, but he continued, "Then you'll make one according to these dimensions. The lady is building her house around this window!"

A father and son (English settlers) erected the building and, though not expert axe-men, made a good solid job of it. Partitions were only seven feet high, to allow of circulation of air and heat. In the gable ends, I had two-foot-square windows, hung on hinges and worked by pulleys. These proved a real blessing in hot weather.

Conversely, this lack of ceilings brought about a surprising, and very picturesque, condition in winter. Heat from the big box-stove warmed up the roof, snow melted and dripped from the eaves, causing enormous icicles to form. But even they (melted) were welcome on a particularly heavy wash-day.

Then, for the inside "finishing", I was fortunate in finding an old man named Carrier, native of Dover, who had been a ship's carpenter. For a small salary, plus room and board, he was willing to do this work and act as chore-man. His work was first-class and we had lots of fun designing cupboards, book-cases for each side of the windows, all of which were installed lengthwise, with sash sliding both ways, and an Old Country dresser. This was our "piece de résistance." For the uninitiated, let me explain that this item of furniture is in no way related to dressing – in any form. With shelved cupboards below, drawers beneath the wide top, then graduated narrow shelves up to wall-height, it provides a hold-all for every requisite of the table: linen, silver cutlery, glass, china – in fact, everything but food. It is much roomier and more in keeping with a backwoods home than any sideboard. I designed mine with sliding doors, panelled drawers (both fitted with frosted brass handles) and, like all the woodwork, painted ivory.

Incidentally, years later, when finally leaving Silver Mountain, I sold some of the heavier furniture to neighbours. A young Finnish woman came to look at the cook-stove, and promptly fell in love with the dresser! "But it is not for sale," I said. "My mother wants it for her home in the city."

"Well, please, sometime you want to sell, you write to me? I come down and buy."

Nine years later, I kept that promise, not even knowing if the woman was still there, or alive, even. She arrived on the next train, with money in hand.

Because, as previously mentioned, hewing of the wall-logs was not of the expert variety, the living-room walls were hung with a soft green casement-cloth, bedrooms with embossed pale-tint building paper.

There were inevitable times when Carrier and I did not see eye-to-eye on the way in which things were to be done. As a true artisan, he would say, "But that is not the usual way of doing (or having) it," to which I would reply, "I don't like it the usual way! I want things different. Besides, we must save every possible inch of space. It will be a new experience, for all of us, 'making do' with a combined living-dining-room-kitchen. That's why I chose sliding doors for the dresser. That's why the bedrooms will have no doors – just curtains." This he evidently considered very eccentric. However, my orders were naturally followed, even though reluctantly.

Another settler, who had been a plasterer before taking to bushwhacking, built the concrete chimney. It puzzled me that so few people had this protection, when winter temperatures called for huge wood fires in cast-iron heaters, the pipes from which would sometimes become almost red-hot. Surprising, too, that nobody used storm doors or windows, considered essential in district cities.

Carrier and I worked like beavers in anticipation of the family's arrival. Then came word that, on account of illness, they wouldn't be coming until the following summer.

According to his own story, the old Doverite was a very devout Anglican. Early the next Spring, it was hinted he would much like to attend Easter services at St. John's Church, where he had some years ago, voluntarily, built the new altar. I gladly spared him and as a reward for faithful work, bought him a new brown suit, boots and Fedora hat and gave him some cash.

Whether he was as good a Churchman as suggested, I don't know. Apparently he had a most enjoyable time, returning on the day appointed, so gloriously intoxicated he literally rolled off the rear end of the train into a deep, muddy ditch; and peacefully lay there. Utterly disgusted at the fate of the nice new suit, I got two men to retrieve the old man, carry him across the tracks and dump him in a hay-shed to sober up. I knew some of his friends, when I was out of sight, would rescue him and take him over to the boarding-house.

One day, an old bachelor, when calling for his mail, thrust a bit of paper in my hand, remarking, "Maybe this'll come in handy, if you're aimin' to buy a pianner for yer Ma. Won it in a contest one o' them music stores been runnin' in the Chronicle." It was a $50 certificate on the purchase of any piano in stock.

"How very thoughtful of you, Andy! A lot of men, if they didn't want it themselves, would have thrown it in the stove. Yes, the idea has lurked in the back of my mind, and this may help to decide." It did and I bought one.

The delay in coming of my people offered an opportunity

to build a frame extension to The Bungalow, as I called the home. This was 12x26 feet, providing a large kitchen with pantry at one end and suficient space to partition off a small bedroom at the other end, if needed. There was also an eight-foot square cement basement and a sink. I was fondly hoping that some day I'd be able to wangle running water, or at least an indoor pump. Neither dream ever materialized, though both were experimented on.

When this addition was all but complete, and I daily looked for the wire giving the great date, the neighbours gave me a surprise house-warming party. It happened that day that a railway bridge had been partially destroyed by fire, and the local couldn't return to the city until the bridge and building gang had repaired the damage. During the afternoon, the train crew (all four of them) came up to see if they could be of any help. They installed the last window but told me nothing of the proposed party.

As I relaxed, after a specially busy day, I could hear the subdued voices of some visitors just approaching. Then in swarmed practically all the neighbours within a radius of two miles, having been notified, according to custom for impromptu affairs, by a young fellow on horseback.

The women provided delectable refreshments and, using both living room and kitchen, there was ample space for dancing, three or four sets at a time. To the delight of everyone, one of the train crew was an accomplished pianist, so (as a man remarked) "For once we have real music!", which seemed like a slight on the usual type, violin, accordion or mouth-organ, cheerfully guiding the "light fantastic". No one departed before 1 a.m. when all joined in singing, "For She's a Jolly Good Fellow".

Thus, after many vicissitudes, I was the proud possessor of not only a homestead, but a home.

CHAPTER TEN

The Family Arrives

The bungalow was built and partially furnished, a reliable handy-man established. All I lacked was the telegram announcing the family's landing on Canadian soil. But there lurked a jinx!

Knowing Mother's propensity, owing to a heart condition, for missing trains, ships and other means of transportation, I had suggested that, as time drew near for their departure, cabling from England was unnecessary. There would be ample time for me to meet them in Port Arthur if they wired from Montreal, where they planned to stay a couple of days.

Mother and Vera were to be accompanied by a former maid, Elizabeth, who had served my mother for 23 years, first as a nurse and later as cook. I had been asked to "please look at for a property for her at Silver Mountain, suitable for poultry-farming". Personally I'd a poor opinion of Western Ontraio, with temperatures ranging from 40 below zero at times, for such an endeavour. However, she wanted to be near, and I secured a deeded farm with good log house and outbuildings; gathered together sufficient furniture and a cat. I knew Elizabeth would not be happy anywhere without at least one cat!

How is it, I wonder, that for some people, nothing ever runs along in the orthodox, cut-and-dried way? If may add to the spice of life, but can be awkward, at times.

During the three-and-a-half years I'd been in charge of the station, all wires had been phoned to me by the despatcher. This important one arrived by mail – the day after the family had reached Port Arthur! The man who was to take charge during my few days' absence finished sorting the mail, while I hurriedly changed to catch the returning local. Most trains on branch lines, 40-odd years ago, were known as "mixed". Directly behind the engine would come a number of box and flat-cars – empty coming, and loaded on a later trip with timber of some sort. Then came the way-freight, baggage car and lastly the lone passenger-coach.

It was October; there had been a lot of rain, and I noticed that the engineer drove cautiously, particularly through clay-cuts, where the road bed was apt to be squishy. About ten miles on our way, there was a sudden bumpy, jerky motion, followed by the squeal of brakes. No mistaking the signs – we were off the track! Not an unusual occurrence on this line. Yes, everything was off except the engine, though only two cars were ditched.

When the first excitement subsided, I approached the conductor. "How could you! I've been living up here for four years and this is the first time I've been in a hurry to get to town!"

"Don't worry! I'll get you there, even if we have to leave the train behind," was his cheerful response.

There was only one other woman passenger aboard, and before we quite knew it, we were both being assisted up into the engine-cab. Men were accommodated on top of the coal in the tender until an empty boxcar could be picked up from a siding. It even looked as though we might reach our destination ahead of time, there being few stops and no switching. But no such luck! At the Junction, our Conductor politely but firmly announced that the Superintendent disapproved of his delivering passengers on the engine. He would give us passes on the main-line train, due shortly. So, while cooling our heels unti it came along, I phoned the Mariaggi Hotel where I had engaged a suite of rooms. My folk were not there! What next?

Fortunately, Vera met the main-line passenger train, as well as the local that had failed to materialize; otherwise, I'd have had to hunt for them. "We're at the Algoma," she announced, when greetings were over, "where you usually stay when in the city, and are most comfortable. They've given us the honeymoon suite, and are treating us like royalty!". It was only a block from the station, and in a very short time we were celebrating the reunion with a quart of champagne, served in person by the proprietor, a jovial Irishman, who, at Mother's invitation, graciously assisted in its consumption.

Elizabeth retired early. Although a berth had been reserved for her, on the trip from Montreal, she had stubbornly refused to retire, preferring to sit up all night. She was too discreet to say why, and we decided she must consider it improper with men sleeping in the same coach.

After the departure of our genial host, the three of us started simultaneously asking questions. My first was, "But how do you happen to be at the Algoma?".

Mother explained, "We waited at the C.P.R. Station until practically everyone had departed, thinking you had been detained and might appear at any moment. Then a very courteous man presented himself, offering assistance. After explaining there was no train from Silver Mountain until the following day, he suggested this hotel as quieter than the big one near the station. Then he brought us all over in his car."

At this point the two smiled at one another, as though enjoying a secret joke. Then Vera said, "We found out later he is an undertaker! A unique welcome, don't you think?".

This was the first "gathering of the clan" for nine years, and talk naturally extended into the small hours. No need to be up early next morning to catch a train; there wouldn't be one going our way for three days. When that time arrived, the trip proved highly entertaining to the newcomers, even without the excitement of derailment. They derived quite a kick from identifying unusual sights I had written of, perhaps the funniest being an old box-car, converted into a waiting-room alongside the platform of a "flag-stop". The Railway Company had thoughtfully provided it with a small wood heater, so that passengers, having, occasionally, to wait hours for a train, might not freeze. But the stove-pipes had long ago been stolen, rendering the stove useless. On this particular day, a large cow had taken her position in the doorway, calmly chewing her cud and eyeing the train with mild interest. Another novelty was the name of a wayside stopping-place, which the Scottish train-agent elongated into a wail, "NON....NA...Loo-oo-o-o-o!".

"Sounds like a South Sea Island," remarked Mother, and I explained it was an abbreviation of Northern Land & Lumber Company – No. La. Lu.

It was pitch dark when we pulled into our station, where awaited the only conveyance in the district capable of carrying us all at once (other than a wagon). Built on the lines of a buggy, but long, with two seats, it had been known in its youth as a "democrat". From whence it had been unearthed, no one enquired, but it was driven, with much pride, by the son of the boardinghouse keeper, and we assuredly were glad of its capaciousness when heading for The Bungalow. To Britishers, travelling along a narrow, not-too-smooth road, downhill, over a wooden river-bridge and up a steep grade, in complete darkness, was something of an adventure. Bush horses don't seem to need headlights!

I had previously sent home a floor-plan of the original log building, never having mentioned the large addition at the back. Carrier, the handy man, left in charge during my absence, had the main portion fully lighted and, of course, stoves going, but kept discreetly out of sight, knowing I had planned a couple of surprises. First was the piano, which caused great jubilation. The second (and this not planned by me) was real floors. They had actually imagined that all bush houses had dirt floors! The third as when I opened what as supposed to be the back door, and disclosed the 12x26-foot addition.

Carrier, a capable cook, had an excellent dinner almost ready to serve. I might here mention that Elizabeth and he took an instant dislike to one another, which they never overcame. It was doubtless jealousy on her part. Although no longer in Mother's service, she evidently felt that the culinary department was hers by right, so long as she chanced to be around.

It is difficult to describe the joy we all felt at being together again after the long years of separation, nor to express my personal delight of finding both Mother and Vera not only genuinely intrigued with their surroundings, but enjoying the novelty of life in the wilds. Both animal lovers, either of the tame or wild variety, they certainly had some odd "introductions" to the latter during their first year at the Bungalow! Even I, before coming West, had no first-hand knowledge of these denizens of the forest, other than black squirrel in Queen's Park, Toronto.

Well, the jinx having apparently departed, I left my nearest and dearest in Carrier's care, departing for the station, accompanied by Elizabeth, so that I would be ready for early morning duties. The railway was experimenting in having the Pee Dee leaving town in the afternoon, stay overnight at Whitefish, and leave at an unconscionable time next morning. I had to be up at 5:30 a.m. to put the mail bags on the train! Fortunately, we were now served only bi-weekly.

Carrier, I knew, would perform his duties capably and cheerfully until his term of office was up, which would be after everyone was sorted out between the three abodes, Bungalow, Station and Poultry-farm-to-be.

I kept Elizabeth with me at the Station for several days, feeling she might be lonesome on the farm I had secured for her; also with the idea of initiating her into the secrets of cooking by virtue of a wood stove! We had long chats on old days, and I reminded her of the Derbyshire "sayings" she used to quote.

"You know, Elizabeth, there was one we could never, as children, understand. You would say, 'Oh, I can always do without what I can't have.' Many, many times, since coming to live in the bush, I've realized its truth, and applied it. One learns from necessity to do without."

I gained the impression during these talks, that she was not so keenly interested in poultry-keeping as in being near my sister, to whom she had always been most devoted. Indeed, coming to us as nurse when Vera was just a month old, it was naturally a case of "my baby". We both had a hearty laugh over one of these reminscences, in particular.

Because Father had to be away from home – sometimes for fairly long periods – in various parts of Europe and even India, Mother had always had complete control of our manners and morals. One thing impressed upon us, when very young, was not to tell tales on one another. If we were naughty (and knew it) or broke something she valued, we must go straight to her and "confess"; then she would never be annoyed.

On one occasion, soon after returning from abroad, Father noticed Vera, who was only four, slashing some prized flowers in the garden with a stick. He mentioned this to Mother, and Vera was sent for to be reprimanded. Standing with hands behind her back, she said not a word, then dashed up to the nursery and her dear Elizabeth where she exclaimed, indignantly, "Fancy a g'own up Farver telling tales!".

We never forgot that little incident; Father, particulary, thought it rich, and told many of his married friends.

Over the weekend, Elizabeth was established in her new home – definitely too spacious for one person, but the only available place. In spite of spending a good deal of time with us, she felt lonesome and it wasn't long before she became attracted to a mere two-room cabin on the adjoining property. This wasn't for sale, but we were able to arrange for occupancy. In a way, this move was timely, as Pierre, my foreman, was anxious to bring his wife and young family up from town, and the farm just suited them. Soon we had an old-fashioned barn-raising, when all the neighbours converged and had it completed in one day. Elizabeth did her full share in preparing the two substantial meals, and a big party followed.

Very shortly after this, there was a population explosion. An English couple (I forget the name, but we'll call them Dawes) arrived from the West, where they had been unsuccessfully farming, bringing with them a car-load of belongings, including horse and equipment, feed and household effects. The wife, apparently wishing to impress the settlers, spread a report that in England, her people "kept their own horses and carriages". The first time she came into the store, her accent clearly showed her to be Old Country, I naturally asked her from what part she came. We discovered both had lived in the same suburb of Manchester, where she had been a maid in our Doctor's household. A small world, indeed!

These people gave the impression of being rather hard up, but when I offered Dawes a few days' work, he was "too busy". It was noticed that they spent a good deal of time driving around (it 'was good for the wife's health'), and nearly always arrived at the home they were visiting at meal times, which did not make them too popular.

At train time, I always locked the store until Post Office duties were disposed of. One day, as I busily sorted the mail, Elizabeth, who happened to be in the kitchen, kept making frantic signals to me and pointing out the window. Finally, I stole a few moments to ascertain what this behaviour meant. There was Dawes, with horse and wagon, busily loading up with bags of coal from the dump behind the freight-shed. Knowing, of course, that I was much too fully occupied to see what was going on and not counting on Elizabeth's presence he was taking his opportunity.

I slipped quietly through the shed, opened the sliding rear door with a bang, and said: "Mr. Dawes, that coal belongs to the railway company, and you must know it. Put back every ounce you've taken!". Besides several sacks full, he had stowed huge lumps beneath the seat. With jaw dropped and a thunderstruck look on his countenance, he silently began to obey. I continued, "If you had asked me, I might have given you some, but not now.". Elizabeth was jubilant.

I was not actually being deprived of fuel, but I strongly objected to the method of acquistion. Before taking possession of the premises, I had a good sized bin built in a rear corner of the freight-shed, and had the new supply deposited there. Who wanted to dig after snow-storm for coal? Roughing it was alright, but there was no sense in putting up with avoidable discomfort.

Photos

Photo credits: Thunder Bay Historical Museum Society; Elinor Barr; Burton Brown; Elle Andra-Warner.

Dorothea at the dock.

Photo courtesy of Burton Brown/Elle Andra-Warner.

Dorothea Mitchell, the engineer.

Silver Mountain station as it was when occupied by the author.

Silver Mountain Station from the 1950s after it had fallen into a state of disrepair.

Silver Mountain station as it is today.

Dorothea's pets Jacko and Bambi.

Dorothea and her dog.

Pee Dee engine.

Miners. Left to right: John Tretheway; Thomas Curran; Oliver Daunais; Joseph Manitoshen; unknown; Richard Tretheway.

Dorothea's Sister.

Silver Mountain station 1899.

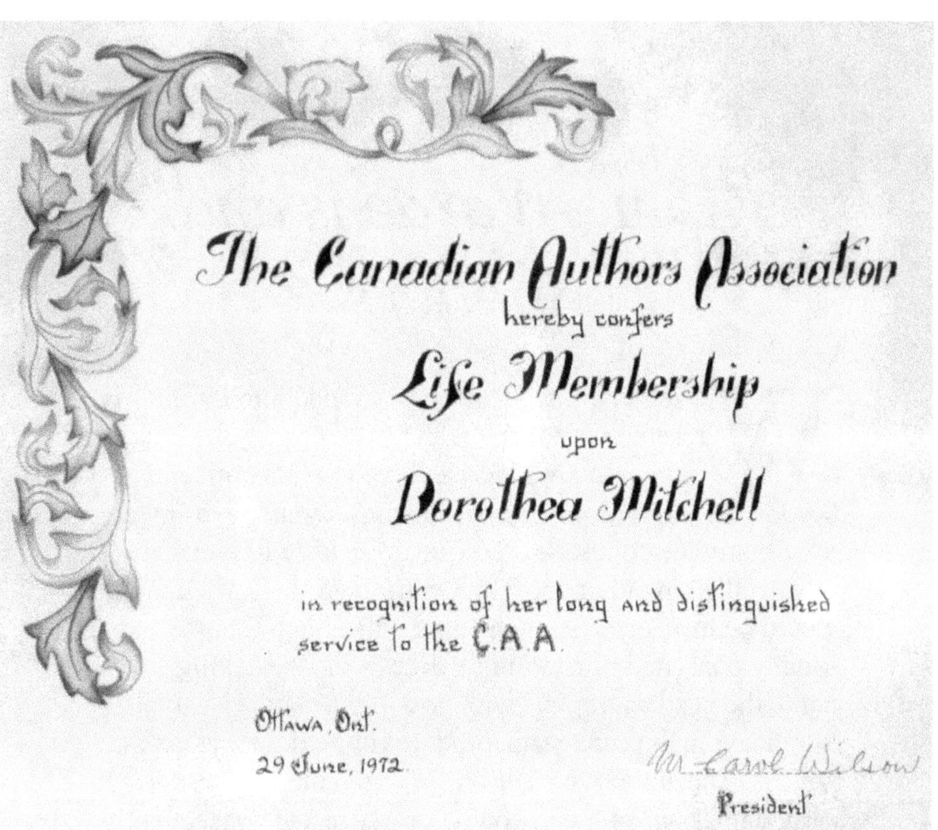

Dorothea Mitchell's honourary lifetime membership in the *Canadian Authors Association* for her publication of this book, "Lady Lumberjack", and also for her work within the organization.

Plaque courtesy of Elinor Barr.

CHAPTER ELEVEN

Game-Wardens and Spotters

We settlers in the Northern wooded interior bitterly resented the fact – justifiably, I thought, – that our game laws were evolved at Government headquarters in Toronto, where no consideration was given to our climatic conditions. Maybe these wise law-makers preferred taking their sport in the mild weather, when there would be little or no snow to cope with! Such "sport" usually consisted of shooting a deer or moose, taking home the head as trophy (with possibly a choice steak or two) leaving the carcass to either rot or be devoured by wolves. The authorized season for big game was set for early winter, when meat would not freeze and consequently spoiled within a few days.

Under these circumstances, it was not surprising that most of the settlers broke the law in obtaining the fresh meat nature supplied, and to which they felt fully entitled. Every decent person, I am convinced, respected the breeding season and despised those who killed for the sake of killing. We killed to eat.

About every twenty miles or so, some reliable settler living near the railroad would be appointed game-warden. Nobody felt resentful when caught by one of these; they had to justify the small wages received from a beneficient government. What we did resent were the "spotters", neighbours with whom we had to do business and to simulate friendly (?) intercourse. They earned a percentage of the fine imposed, and for this reason were keener than the regular wardens. One of them, getting wind of a "kill", would casually drop in around the dinner hour, knowing he would be invited to eat, since that was the invariable custom in the woods, and the kindly host would know what to expect!

Among other regulations, it was illegal to carry fire-arms on Sunday.

One Saturday, it was necessary for me to visit some sub-contractors at a distance of about nine miles, and, having no driver at the time, I was obliged to walk. Starting out in the early afternoon, it would be dark before I reached the home at which I would spend the night, so I carried my shot-gun. Two miles from home, I had to pass the farm of one of these unpopular "spotters". He must have glimpsed me at a distance and was leaning on the barn-yard gate as I drew near. I paused, and in the friendliest manner we passed the time of day and asked after one another's families. Then, with kindly interest, came the query, "And where might you be heading for, miss?". I told him.

"My! That's a long walk for a lady! Maybe someone will be after driving you back?".

"No," I replied. "I don't mind distance when the roads are so well packed and I'm wearing moccassins. Mrs. Denny will put me up and I'll trek back tomorrow."

Although he looked me straight in the face throughout this brief conversation, I felt a third eye on my gun!

People will tell you it is never quite dark when the ground is snow-covered. But on a moonless, starless night, with tall timber on either side of the road, there is mighty little illumination around one's feet. This was demonstrated as, nearing the end of my hike, I came to forked roads. Not being certain which one to take, I had to strike matches to determine the more travelled. Luckily, I hit on the right one!

Inspection of sub-contractors' progress was done in the forenoon of Sunday and shortly after dinner I started home by a different route, bagging five or six birds on the way. Neighbours who told me, next day, that the "spotter" had set out to meet me (and my gun) Sunday afternoon, exulted in his having missed me. I hoped he enjoyed the walk!

As I may have already mentioned, our local ran through to North Lake every Wednesday, returning next day. It was a most beautiful spot, where, despite rather meagre population, I already had several good friends, who always welcomed guests. Only three families lived there, besides the section-gang and a charming old Irishman named Rooney, who occupied the station and kept in touch with the despatcher by phone (the place was too dead to necessitate an Agent).

Once in a while, during summer, I would make this trip, if only to enjoy more rugged surroundings than my own. On one such occasion, in August, I stayed with a trapper and his wife. Wild raspberries were in profusion, so I borrowed a twenty-pound pail and headed for a patch they told me of, a mile down the track. Just as I left the house, the husband came after me and said, "There are lots of birds there, too! Would you like to have this .22? The barrel is a bit bent, but maybe you can handle it."

"Thanks!" I said, "if it doesn't back-fire, I'll take a chance."

"I've no shells," he continued, "but I'm pretty sure Mr. Rooney can give you some."

On the way to the berry-patch, I dropped in at the station and borrowed five or six shells. Greatly to my surprise, the bent barrel was no detriment (perhaps my eye was crooked that day!) and in a very short time ammunition was exhausted. This was far more fun than picking berries! Hurrying back, I dashed through the waiting-room to the office beyond, saying: "Oh, Mr. Rooney, could you let me have a few more shells? I've used those – "

"Sh-h-h-h-h!" he hissed, "that's the game-warden sitting in the waiting-room!"

"Well," said I, "it's too late now. He must have heard what I said. And, anyway, my pail full of birds is staring at him from the other bench. I may as well be hung for ten birds, as five."

As, armed with a fresh supply of ammunition, I returned to my bird-patch, the game-warden was gazing out of the window, never even glancing in my direction. But he was strange to me, and there was no knowing how he might react.

However, next morning as I boarded the train, he handed me some money, asking that I send him two boxes of 22-longs on next Wednesday's train – a tactful way of letting me know that he, too, was shooting things. I knew it would not be rabbits, because they, like oysters, are no good unless there is an "r" in the month.

There has long been an unwritten law in Ontairo, as in other provinces across the Dominion, that no one kills the porcupine. That is, unless he were lost in the woods. Traditionally, it is the only edible wild-meat procurable without a gun; a well-directed stone or a good whack on the nose with a stick will lay him cold. The porcupine, feeling himself amply protected by his quill armour against physical attack by man or beast, never runs away. He considers sticks and stones harmless, and of course knows nothing about guns.

A lost person, in my opinion, might readily starve while searching for such a meal, for I saw only about a dozen of these prickly little fellows during as many year' residence in this wooded area. They struck me as rather sinister. Somehow one does not picture them climbing trees, nor

swimming – but they do both. They'll sit on the limb of a
tree and glare unblinkingly at one with a half sulky, half
belligerent look.

One summer, I bought and carefully carried home from
the city a dozen tomato plants and tended them with great
care. Because the weather was hot, I protected each plant
during the day with an empty 50-lb butter box, tipping
these off at night to allow some air and early-morning
light. They were progressing splendidly when, at five one
morning, my Mother awakened me by calling: "Oh, do
come quickly! There's a porcupine eating your precious
tomato plants."

Was I mad! Scrambling out of bed, I grabbed my gun
and shot it from the door. It hadn't eaten the plant, it turned
out, but had paddled them all flat, going from one box to
another, licking the inside. Like most wild animals, they
love salt. Having at that time no idea what good eating
it would be, nor the vaguest notion how to get rid of the
quills, I just dug a hole and buried the brute.

Practically every family kept at least one dog, and we
all dreaded the visit of a porcupine. Seeing one of them sit
there, unafraid, a dog invariably attacks, and as invariably
gets the worst of the encounter. One neighbour owned a
valuable bull dog who fought to the finish, as any dog of
his breed will. His eyes, tongue and throat were full of
quills and it was hopeless to help him; the poor animal had
to be destroyed on the spot.

But it was not until several yers later, when I moved to
the city, I discovered the ability of the porcupine to swim.
Having acquired a small island with summer cottage on one
of the inland lakes, I had as guest one weekend a friend's
little dog, a Boston Bull. "Mitzi" was contentedly playing
outdoors while I did the morning's work within. Suddenly
the atmosphere was rent by the most blood-curdling

screams – not howls nor barks, but terrified repeated
screams! I rushed out. Near the back steps was a trembling
Mitzi, eyes bulging, ears flattened back, teeth bared and
every hair on her spine bristling. A yard or so from her sat
a lethargic looking porcupine, over from the mainland on
a friendly visit, staring at the terrified dog. Mitzi, far too
cowardly to start a scrap, suffered no damage except to her
nerves.

CHAPTER TWELVE

The Musical Dog

During the course of many years, I have owned dogs of varied breed and diverse characteristics. Only once, though, have I met one that was naturally musical.

It was while visiting on a ranch that my host presented me with a few-weeks-old Collie pup, a mere ball of fluff, with the remarks, "He should make a good dog. He's the only one of a litter of five to survive an unscheduled plunge into the well. His mother is pedigreed, too."

The journey home entailed two stop-overs, travel by three railroads and sundry car-rides. That pup slept through everything, except feeding times! Toby (as I named him) grew up extremely intelligent, most obedient and my inseparable companion; not in any way temperamental, as blue-blooded dogs frequently are.

As soon as Toby was old enough, his favourite pastime was chasing rabbits – without much success. I went after them, too, but with a gun (one of the occasions on which we could not work in partnership) and I thought it rather wonderful that I had merely to say the word "no", and he would sit in the road and sorrowfully watch my departure. Possibly, he sensed that after my lonely excursions he had rabbit for supper!

When only about six months old, I took him down to the river for a swim. The banks were steep and cattle had been watering at the only convenient approach, making it muddy. For this reason, I hung my towel and the light raincoat I'd worn over my suit on some nearby bushes. Before I was many yards from shore, Toby was howling dolefully and

frantically racing around in circles. It is inconceivable that
he remembered seeing his little brother and sisters drown;
yet he was obviously terrified of the water.

Presently there was silence. Not even a bark. Returning
to shore, I could see no sign of my belongings. Then I
discovered Toby, in his frenzy, had torn them from the
bushes, trampled them in the mud and disappeared! The next
time we headed for the river, his manner was calm. Having
apparently decided it was his duty to save me, he dashed
in immediately and swam so close alongside, his claws
scratched my arm.

After Mother and Vera came to live with me, Toby's
allegiance wavered. For some time, I could not understand
this changed attitude. Then I discovered it was music!
When Mother played the piano (and she was a brilliant
performer), he would sit; almost glued to the instrument, a
rapt expression in his eyes.

But the best was yet to come. When Vera brought out
and played her mandolin, he sang! It might best be described
as a "melodious whine". I'm not suggesting that he could
follow a tune, but invariably he raised and lowered his voice
to harmonize with the accompaniment; and my sister played
with a considerable amount of expression, too.

Not long after this talent came to light, we had a house-
guest who also played the mandolin. Naturally we boasted
of our unusual dog, and Vera, thinking to give the visitor
a thrill, handed over her instrument. Unhappily, this girl's
playing was of the "tinkle-tinkle" variety. Toby sat perfectly
rigid, with nose tilted and mouth tight shut. Presently,
without altering his position, he slewed his eyes around
towards us, expressing unmistakably: "Expect me to sing to
THAT?".

This Collie, in various other ways, showed
extraordinarily human reactions. When quite young, Toby

was taught to follow only the garden paths, never to run over flowers or vegetables. Early one morning, hearing the tantalizing chatter of a chipmunk at the far side of the garden, he glanced up at the windows (like a small boy) to see if anyone were watching; then dashed helter-skelter over everything! I pretended not to see this little escapade.

The following spring, we acquired some tame lop-eared rabbits. Until the garden was planted, they were allowed their freedom and associated in a friendly manner with the family cats. However, aware of Toby's propensity for hunting rabbits, I thought it advisable to introduce him to them formally. Keeping my hand on his collar, I stroked the newcomers, saying "nice pussie". He did not even look my way, but his expressoin plainly said, "Is the woman crazy?.... But if she thinks they're cats, I'd better pretend they are.". Whether it was my calling them ''pussies", or the fact that the rabbits showed no fear of him (as wild ones would), one can but conjecture. The fact remains that, after that initial introduction, Toby never molested them.

Vera made him a little forage-cap and cartridge belt, and taught him to salute for his dinner. This he did very smartly, sitting up and raising his right front paw to the side of his head. Very soon he went through the little ritual the moment his plate appeared, not even awaiting the word of command. Then a cousin came to visit us. While greatly intrigued by the performance, he one day (without authority) decided to play a trick on the dog. He held up an empty plate and Toby saluted. The dog's disgust at being fooled was evident, and from that day on, nothing would induce him to perform the customary ceremony until he was satisfied the dinner was on the plate; and we sympathized with him. Incidentally, he was only expected to wear cap and belt on special occasions. The former, he never really liked (it prevented his pricking up his ears), but he would do anything to please his beloved mandolin-lady.

My mother had never been in robust health since living in India. Therefore we felt most thankful in having a girl of fifteen, daughter of an English family recently settled in the district, come three times a week to help in household duties at the Bungalow after Carrier left. I had already engaged an elderly man to do the chores, keeping us supplied with wood and water. Noboby knew why, but from the start Charles called Vera "Miss Ivy" and me "Miss Nora"! With yoke and two pails he carried water up from the creek to a big wooden barrel in the kitchen, fitted with tap – the next best thing to running water. One day he remarked, "I never in all my born days did know such clean people."

Charles had no garden duties, but showed marked interest (if not disapproval) in my activities. Potatoes I set in the British way, about fifteen inches apart and in rows, which he considered peculiar. "Me, I always set mine in hills."

Here was a challenge!

"I think they have more room to spread, if single," I said. "Howeve, we'll prove it. I'll give you the exact weight in the same potatotes. You plant them in hills, alongside mine, and we'll see who gets the best crop." Everything grew well in this virgin soil. When dug, mine was the heavier crop. Seeing his disappointed expression, I felt sorry I had suggested the contest.

One of the delights of family life then was the opportunity to encourage a community spirit. I'd no time for such activities when alone. It was fun introducing activities other than dances, which was all the local people had known thus far. Dominion Day Sports went extremely well, despite the fact that most of the youngsters were too shy to take part in events arranged for them. An appreciation party, with handsome gifts, for a worthy woman who was known for hastening to a sick neighbour, day or night, when needed met with great enthusiasm; a picnic to one of the islands on Whitefish Lake. Even a raffle caused excitement.

In talking with an old Scottish couple one day, Vera chanced to mention that I had taught Highland dancing both in England and in Toronto. After that, every time there was a dance they insisted that I don my kilt and give them the Fling and various reels. Luckily we had a fine Scottish fiddler who could duplicate the bagpipes in marvellous manner.

Because most of the poplar grew on the farther end of my land, it was found more profitable to move the mill to that area, rather than the logs. Not very long after this took place, a lad came into the station and said, "It looks as though the sawdust pile, where your mill used to be, is burning."

Sure enough, a strong wind had fanned sparks into flames that were travelling in the direction of the Bungalow. Sending word to the mill-gang, who couldn't see the smoke from the new location, I locked up and hurried home. The water supply was too meagre to be of any use; it was a matter of beating out or stamping out small fires that were smouldering in leaves and moss. Trees just burned.

Eleven of us, nine men, Vera and I, worked the rest of that day and all night, Mother spending much of her time in making sandwiches and coffee. The soles of our shoes were nearly burned through. Wet blankets were spread on the portion of the roof where spars were falling, and two favourite shade-trees in front of the dwelling had to be felled; a portion of the garden fence was burnt, too. Not a very pleasant experience, but results might have been a great deal more serious. One can at least fight fire, while a flood can be absolutely relentless.

CHAPTER THIRTEEN

Unpremeditated Acquisition

Big contracts were beginning to fade, and after the timber for Breakwater had been shipped, camp was struck and teams disposed of. On my homestead, as on other discarded mining-claims, practically all the best timber had been stolen, but I still had a quantity of poplar, not usually marketable. Then came the chance to sell even it, as lumber.

I got in touch with the Jackson brothers, owners of the very efficient portable mill that had cut for me on the timber limit. An agreement was arrived at regarding price per thousand feet for sawing; I was to employ men for cutting and hauling the logs.

When the appointed time came – no mill!

Then a letter from the firm in the East from whom these men had bought the mill, seven years ago, said that nearly $1,000 was still owing. Under the circumstances, they could not allow it to be moved from the Jackson property until they had a guarantee from me to pay, directly to them, $1.00 for every thousand feet cut. Here was a predicament! I'd already signed my contract for a certain number of car loads and many logs were already cut.

The Jacksons couldn't do otherwise than agree. So, piece by piece, the mill was set up by Beaver Creek, just below the site of the Bungalow and a camp built on a clearing a few hundred feet back. I'd had about half an acre fenced in for gardens, but could not use it because of the road.

But troubles were not at an end. The brothers couldn't agree even on trivial matters. One would come in and ask me to order a certain type of teeth for the circular saw (I'd always thought they were stationary); later the other would come in and want a different brand. Finally, they appeared together. Dick, the older, was the spokesman. "Miss Mitchell, with that $1.00 per thousand deducted for the mill manufacturer, we're not able to make this job pay."

"That's rather awkward for me," I replied. "As you know, I signed my contract on the understanding that you would do the cutting." They glanced at one another rather sheepishly.

Then Jim said, hesitantly:

"I don't suppose you'd consider taking over the mill yourself? We'd be satisfied with a few hundred dollars cash, if you assume the balance owing. We should never have bought it, in the first instance. There isn't enough timber in our locality to keep it busy, and it's been nothing but worry."

And that is how I came to be a sawmill owner! Like so many other things, it was wished upon me by King Circumstance. I didn't really mind. It was known to be the best portable in the neighbourhod, 35 h.p.

By "keeping it busy" I managed to clear off the entire debt in twelve months, largely because I was able to secure a first-class top-sawyer, who was also a certified stationary engineer. A man, Walters, by name, came seeking the job directly after I took over the mill and remained for years.

Around this time, I was asked to supply two cars of a peculiar type of lumber for making coal-doors for railway cars – a man down the line being short on his contract. It had to be in 9-foot lengths and rough-edged; that is, the bark still on. In addition, a certain amount of 1"x 4" had to be included, edged in customary fashion, for "stays". Not having ever cut this rough stuff before, none of my mill employees had a notion how to scale it. I had to evolve a system, and myself pile it in the box-cars. Apparently my method worked, for the consignees told me there was on each car a little more than they were billed for.

As outcome of this small assignment (done to oblige a fellow in the same line of business) the men who were making the doors for one of the railway companies came up to see me soon after. Because my two cars were the only ones shipped on time, which kept their men busy, instead of hanging around with nothing to do, and everything was up to specifications, they were offering me the full contract of 25 carloads for next season. I accepted, and never had reason to regret it, even though I had to stack every board of it myself. The total contract amounted to $7,870 and it was not once necessary to collect. As each car was unloaded, a cheque was deposited to my bank account.

Most families living in the area, even with no pretension to farming, kept a pig for the purpose of having a supply of first-class pork during the winter. With this in mind, it would be unthinkable to make a pet of the animal; yet the one who hands out the feed is naturally looked upon as a sort of "good companion".

Until becoming acquainted with the species, I shared the common impression that pigs were stupid animals. They are undoubtedly stubborn. Like certain humans, they know what they want, and stick to their guns! But I won't let anyone tell me, now, that they lack intelligence. Poke, our first, had his pen at the Bungalow, and when released, prior to seeding of the garden, spent most of the day contentedly roaming the woods "rooting" and merely showing up at meal-time.

One day, however, when I failed to arrive at the usual luncheon hour because of the train's late arrival, Poke came to look for me. Thereafter he made a practice of following quite regularly and caused much amusement to the train crew and passengers by answering his name. He never learned, fortunately, to mount steps! If bored, he would return home alone.

One one occasion, Poke demonstrated a dog-like trait that I would never have believed pigs possessed. I was piling some rough-edged lumber on a flat-car that had to be shipped the following day and again was late for a meal. Poke came looking for me. But though I called his name repeatedly, he failed to discover my whereabouts, glancing in every direction but up. Then, with nose glued to the ground, he "scented" me all the way to a house two hundred yards away, where I had been called for a cup of tea, earlier in the afternoon.

Once, when obliged to go to the city on business and fearing that Poke might follow, I asked my mother to give him something to eat at the back door, while I departed from the front. This fooled him. But on my return, two days later, there he was – waiting to welcome me at the station.

Reaching home, Mother greeted us with: "My dear! I'm afraid Poke must have been killed by the train. He followed you after all, and has not been home since!"

"On, no!" I replied. "He's here – and full of pep."

Naturally I instituted inquiries as to his whereabouts during my absence. That pig had never left the vicinity of the station, except to scrounge meals from the section-gang or from the boarding-house, for two whole days and nights! Possibly that constitutes "dumb" devotion, but it is assuredly of the intelligent type.

Most of our friendly enemies, as I dubbed the four-legged wild varities, depended, I already knew, upon their sense of smell to detect and avoid natural adversaries; some on hearing; few on vision. The hedgehog, of course, fears neither man nor beast!

Though rabbits raided our vegetable patch, the larger quadrupeds – moose, deer, bear, coyote and fox – kept their distance. The thing we really objected to was the coyotes' occasional blood-curdling "serenades" late at night.

My only encounter with a big black bear was meeting one on a narrow trail. We both stopped in our tracks. Quickly deciding that, should I turn and run, he would probably chase me; also, that a bear climbs a tree with much more agility than I, my best bet would be to stare him out of countenance. It worked! After glaring at one another for a few minutes, he took off into the wods.

Another bit of early aquired knowledge, which proved most useful, was the fact that the only night-prowlers that would approach a light were deer and rabbits – both perfectly harmless. This meant that the carrying of alighted lantern (through no fault of its own!) failed me. Returning from a neighbour's home a few miles from mine, a short cut necessitated the climbing of a snake fence. Carefully depositing the lantern on the far side, I was preparing to follow it when my collie hopped over ahead of me and tipped over the lantern, extinguishing it! And no matches! Coyotes were around, but kept their distance. Incidentally, dogs are desperately afraid of them, so afford no protection. I have heard, on good authority, that neither wolves nor coyotes attack a female canine; but it would be hard to make them realize this.

Long before my years of pioneering ended, I was firmly convinced that most of the smaller species of wildlife are very definitely guided by instinct. They obviously know where they will not be molested. How, otherwise, can one account for the following instances, all personally experienced?

A weasel, adopting itself into the family, provided

great amusement by its antics, particularly in repeated and vain efforts to life hens' eggs frpm a deep bowl. He would stand on his hind legs, reach in with his paws, swearing lustily over non-success as each egg slipped back again, yet never cracking one! We naturally did not attempt to make a pet of this uninvited guest. He just came and went at his pleasure, usualy while the choreman carried in the wood and water. But eventually the little chap became so boldly mischievous, we were obliged to banish him.

Our next visitor, fortunately for only a brief call, was a lynx (wild cat), curled up early one morning on the front verandah, leaning aginst the screen door. Mother, having no idea of its ferocity, would have tried to stroke it. There was no desire, in this case, either to cultivate the visitor's acquaintance. Seemingly no other home in the district was so "favoured".

Of the smaller-four-legged creatures, chipmunks were decidedly the sauciest. If once fed, they would climb onto window sills and loudly demand more, though making no attempt to come indoors.

For a considerable time a red fox made a practice of escorting me on my way to business each morning, running parallel, but never closer than two yards, and disappearing into the bush as we approached cleared land. Maybe he was lonely. At any rate, he liked being talked to.

But possibly our most unusual uninvited guest was a lady skunk! Our home was of log construction, well "banked" with earth for warmth in winter. Faint movements beneath the floor were at first attributed to one of the cats. Howeve, one moonlight night in summer, my mother glimpsed the pretty, striped form of this skunk heading straight for the banking. And, being an early riser, she also saw the same form scoot across the garden and into the woods. Obviously we had a "roomer"! Well, there was nothing we could do about it, except pray that Madam Skunk would not take fright.

That night, and every night following, a large bowl of warm bread and milk was placed outside the scratched-out entrance. Each morning it was found, licked clean.

In due course, a family of three skunk kitties came out into the garden and played happily with our five domestic kittens. A charming sight! Mama Skunk seemed completely unalarmed by household noises, even to the playing of the piano; then, when she considered her offspring ready for outdoor living, they quietly departed early one morning.

What, other than instinct, could account for such complete trust?

CHAPTER FOURTEEN

Volunteer School and Cookstove-Camera

The term Volunteer School explains itself. A cook-stove-camera is more complicated, and, in order to show how it was a direct result of the former, I'd better start at the beginning.

There were thirteen children of school age within a radius of two miles, and no school within five. Some of us felt that action was called for, and a small committee of kindred spirits was formed. As a start it was decided to levy married men $5.00 and bachelors $2.00. Money was worth a good deal more, in those days. Land in a central position on the main road was donated. Timber for logs was offered and everyone chipped in with volunteer man and team labour.

It didn't take long to raise the 30' x 50' structure which seemed to meet present requirements – particularly since there was no immediate prospect of a teacher! There is considerable square-footage in a half-pitch, gable roof on a building of that size, and we didn't find our "levy" a bit elastic! This little hitch was overcome, however, by buying sufficient lumber for roof and floor, then organizing bi-monthly dances to raise money for the remaining materials – hoping it would not rain too heavily before the tarred roofing was on. It was summer, so nobody minded the lack of windows and door.

These dances proved real community affiars, even the Finnish settlers (usually inclined to "keep to themselves") soon joined in with great gusto and provided their full share of entertainment. We had a ruling that men only paid admission, the women supplying refreshments. Finns were very dignified dancers and their accordian music, always in a minor key, is reminiscent of dirges, but rather intriguing.

About the time the school house was completed, a young Anglican Missionary was appointed to a village about twelve miles distant. I wrote and said we would be able to put him up, if he could arrange to hold service for us, once a week. This he gladly agreed to do, naming Wednesday. As a result of his meeting the people, and becoming interested in our teacher problem, he offered to remain for three days in the middle of the week and take teacher duty. Everyone was delighted at the idea, with the exception of one woman (the one with the largest family, too!) who said "she had got along very well without any 'eddication', and she didn't see why her children couldn't do the same."

Mr. Fraser, or "The Parson", as he was now generally known, was quite distressed, until I told him afterwards that Ma Weston was just taking advantage of having an audience, and that her children would be the first to show up on opening day. They were, the whole flock of them, including the 16-year-old girl. There was even a married woman, the Austrian wife of a Canadian, attending.

Before winter set in, we added a lean-to kitchen to the school-house and two heaters. Then along came Christmas and the biggest party the district had ever seen; there were even special guests from the city. Local parents brought such gifts as they had, those without children donated toys and good things for the 12-foot candle-lit tree, which brought gapes and gasps from the youngsters. Some of them, I'm sure, thought it had grown through the floor especially for the occasion.

Early in our acquaintance, Mr. Fraser had mentioned he

didn't like his boarding place and was planning to "batch"
in a shack. This involved gathering up some furniture and
I offered to lend him a small cookstove. A few weeks later,
chatting one evening, he asked if either my sister or I was
interested in photography. I said I thought I would be, if I
had a camera. To which he responded, "I have a rather good
one, a 3-A folding Browning and I'll be happy to lend it
to you." I thought he was just anxious to reciprocate; but
eventually he suggested a trade, remarking that I had much
better luck with the camera than he, so "how about trading
it for the stove?". Thus, in our family, it became known
as the cookstove-camera. It was, as Mr. Fraser had said, a
good one, having exceptionally fast lens. Immediately, I
became an ardent fan! I bought a little publication entitled
"How to Make Good Pictures" (25c I believe was the
price) and had extraordinary success for a green-horn. I
even tackled the developing and printing for a while but,
lacking running water, it was a tedious job and I reverted
to professional finishing. I gave the camera full credit for
some exceptionally fine action shots it produced such as
birds in flight, children at play, logging operations.

Mother and Vera, so recently out from England, were
naturally anxious to send pictures of their new backwoods
home to folk in the Old Land. Anyone can take good
outdoor scenes; but I still feel proud of the interiors,
by daylight time exposures, with neither electricity nor
flashbulb.

Eventually our nice young volunteer teacher left the
district. Not long after this, the authorities decided to
construct a more modern building and supply a salaried
teacher.

In after years, my cookstove-camera led me into some
odd situations and earned for me one unenviable reputation.
Brownie had never once let me down but the experiment

that surprised me most was far from my own planning or desire. After I had returned to city life, a neighbour lost a very sweet little four-year-old girl. The funeral was to be in the morning and, quite early, an elder sister phoned to say her mother would be grateful if I would take a picture of the little one in her casket.

"I'll try, certainly," I replied, "though I'm not at all sure it will be any good. You see, I have no flashbulb, and time exposures by ordinary electric lighting are usually failures."

I got them to put the most powerful bulb they had (100 W.) in the ceiling fixture and bring me a step-ladder. This I mounted, slanted the camera down towards the casket and gave it 30 seconds – never for a moment expecting anything to show on the film. Indeed, when the resulting picture turned out excellent, I considered it a pure fluke. To me, the whole idea seemed rather weird. But the mother was so happy about it, I had an enlargement made and very faintly tinted, which made the sweet little thing appear to be merely sleeping. It was hung in an honoured place in their living room!

It must have been several months after this occurrence that my phone rang. One of our leading undertakers said in a cheery voice, "Miss Mitchell, I understand you have quite a reputation for taking pictures of the departed?"

"Oh, I hope not!" I exclaimed impulsively.

"This is rather a sad case," he went on. "A Ukrainian widow and young son came to Canada only six months ago. Now the mother has died and the boy very much wants a picture of her. Could you come right away? We'll send a car for you."

Naturally, I went. The casket was set in a bay window, semi-daylight penetrating the lace curtains. Around the room were all the sorrowing friends, none of whom could speak more than a few words in English.

With the same equipment as before, I had just mounted the ladder when, to my horror, the sad-faced son, a lad of 15 or so, indicated that he wished to sit beside the casket and be included! And so it was. This picture, too, came out far beyond expectations, and presumably made the boy happy.

Considering the circumstances, I had been glad to do it, but asked the undertaker to forget, in future, my "reputation" – a reputation earned for me by my valued "cookstove-camera".

CHAPTER FIFTEEN

Let's Have Eggs For Supper

If you who live in city or village are short of eggs, you can run to the corner store. But we were frequently made to realize we were in the backwoods and forty miles from civilization.

When long periods of sub-zero temperatures prevailed and we needed foodstuffs that freezing would depreciate – such as potatoes, onions and eggs – we just waited until "weather permitted". Everything ordered from town would lie in the freight sheds overnight, then travel possibly half a day in a boxcar on its way out. Even toting any disaster by sleigh was bound to end in damage.

Late one February, after an exceptionally severe winter, a phenomenal thaw set in, continuing for nearly a week. Snow was melted, spring creeks broke through, combining to flood rivers on top of several feet of ice. This, naturally, was a great blow to settlers using the river for hauling timber to the railway.

Then an almost-as-surprising cold snap came, freezing this upper flow; not as solid as the original surface, but still sufficiently stable for lighter loads.

One Sunday morning, apropos of nothing, my sister said, ironically, "Let's have eggs for supper!"

"Excellent suggestion!" I responded. "You've given me an idea. Maybe old Bill Kidd will spare us a few, since there won't be a train for three days; and travelling on the river, instead of over Saddleback Hill, there'll be a better chance of getting them home unscrambled."

Old Bill was a cripple, living about five miles up the Whitefish River, who made a living by poultry-keeping, shipping his produce to town. His hens laid when others didn't. And, because of his crippled condition, the train crew carried his eggs on the baggage-car, where they were safe from frost.

In the early afternoon, throwing a couple of blankets into the cutter for the protection of my hoped-for cargo, I set out. Currents being always stronger on bends, and the ice thinner in consequence, I kept close to the river bank. Even at that, there came the occasional sound of a distant crack. We passed a gang of men, cutting spruce boughs and trampling them into spots where the crust was giving. After the night's freeze-up, this would constitute a fairly satisfactory reinforcement.

Then, perhaps a quarter of a mile farther, I noticed an omnious crack – this time at close quarters – and my horse's hoofs begin to sink through. Next, the cutter and I were sinking. Although a high-spirited animal, Prince behaved like a lamb, patiently waiting for me to make the next move. For a few moments I just sat there, quietly talking to him, wondring how much deeper we might sink!

When the watery slush began seeping onto the floorboards of the cutter, Prince remaining stationary, I guessed the solid ice was only about eighteen inches below. Not bad! All the same, action was called for. I stepped gingerly onto the ice, hardly expecting that so near the broken edge it would bear my weight. Surprisingly, it did!

Next, I "halloo-ed" back to the repair gang, who came on the run. This being my first experience of the kind, it was most interesting to watch their method of extricating us. First they trampled the ice down, between us and the shore; then led Prince and the cutter onto the riverbank. I hopped in, and we were on the ice surface again, a few yards ahead, in the matter of minutes. As simple as that.

"Thanks, boys!" I said, "now I'll know what to do, if this happens on the way home, though I don't relish the idea of having to do it in moccasins." They, of course, wore rubber waders.

Old Bill's welcome was hearty: "My, my! But it's nice to have an unexpected visitor, and a lady at that! Haven't seen one in months."

Learning of my errand, he immediately said, "Why, sure you shall have eggs, even if my city order goes short. Was just going out to gether 'em up. How about coming along? Then you'll know they're today's laying." Then, with a chuckle, "And don't you mind if the hens is scared of you. They ain't used to skirts!"

"Oh, that's nothing," I laughed. "When I visited some people, back-of-beyond, some months ago, the children were scared of me. Probably they'd never seen a woman, other than their own mother. They all scooted behind the cookstove! However, when I produced cookies and candy, they decided I was harmless."

Armed with two canes, without which Old Bill could not navigate, we started a round of the hen houses. Never inclined to be backward in seeking information, I learned a good deal on that tour. The first thing that struck me was that, instead of one big house to accommodate the several hundred birds, there were several small ones, maybe housing fifty each. Also, it seemed remarkable that no stoves were used, where 30 degrees below zero was common.

"That's a little secret that not many knows," he told me. "If a hen-house has the proper cubic-foot space to the number of birds, they heat it themselves. Ever put your hand under a settin' hen's wings? It'll 'most burn you! And there's another thing lots of folk don't know. Houses have to be ventilated, too."

I made mental note of all this, and later tried out the old man's methods; next winter, we too had hens that laid, much to the family's delight.

Returning to the shack, in order to wrap and pack the eggs for travel, Old Bill insisted that he make me a cup of tea and "'flap-jacks", both of which proved excellent. While he dexteriously busied himself around the stove, I entertained him with all the current neighbourhood news. Presently he said, "Why don't you never come and see me in the summer? Maybe you don't like the Saddleback Hill?"

"I can't say it impressed me very favourably, the only time I tried it – in summer."

"What happened?" he said, eagerly. "Meet a bear?"

"Much worse than that!" I responded, feelingly. "I was starting out, on foot, to visit some people at the back of the township, when young Glover told me his dad was taking a wagonload of stuff out to their pre-emption, and would gladly give me a lift. It seemed a good idea. Well, we'd no sooner begun to climb the Saddleback trail (its hardly a road!) than John said, 'Here, you take the lines; I want to walk a bit.' It wasn't too bad, going up; they were easy-going old plugs. Once I glanced behind and realized why John wanted to walk. He was taking a swig from a suspicious-looking flask! As soon as we started on the downgrade everything in the wagon began sliding towards the front end, including the seat on which I was perched. It was only by bracing myself against the dashboard that I avoided being thrown onto the horses' backs by the pressure of baled hay behind; under my feet were axes, horseshoes and haywire. I hung onto the lines to the best of my ability, but we descended at an unseemly pace!"

Old Bill's eyes were glistening. "Good job you had the

lines, 'instead of John. He goes to sleep, when he's had a drink or two."

It was dusk when the homeward journey started, and some degrees colder. This was all to the good. Surface ice, softened by the sun, would have hardened again.

Taken by and large, the afternoon had proved highly entertaining, and it was with a feeling of satisfaction that I landed my precious load home, intact – and without personal immersion in the river's icy slush – though two frozen thumbs resulted from the trip, despite fleece-lined leather mitts. For many years following, the very mention of forst would make them split.

Anyway, after being without for several weeks, those eggs for supper certainly tasted good!

CHAPTER SIxTEEN

Fate, Fruit and Fire

Many will recollect that during the early years of the War, the United States showed marked sympathy towards Germany. There were murmured whisperings among Pee Dee settlers, with all section-foremen (except one) either German or Austrian, and an unprotected boundary; "Who knows what may happen?" Actually most of these men were tickled to death to be in Canada, and not obliged to fight!

At Silver Mountain, Andrew, the Section Foreman, was Austrian and his dwelling a comfortable log house. I'd occupied the station for about six years when the Roadmaster made one of his periodic visits, and part of a conversation between the two, on the platform, was overhead and relayed to me.

"But Mister, when no Station Agent here, me I should live in station house."

"Miss Mitchell may not be officially the Agent, but she carries out all the duties."

"My Brotherhood says I have right!"

"Well, you're stronger than Miss Mitchell. Why don't you put her out?" Andrew was nonplussed.

Months later, the Superintendent of the line was up and Andrew approached him; he simply turned on his heel and walked away. But eventually I received a courteous letter from this same official, saying he was "extremely sorry, but the Brotherhood of Railway Maintenance-of-Way Employees insisted that the section-foreman be allowed the station as living quarters." But I was to take my time in vacating the premises. It wasn't exactly nice, having to make way for an Austrian, and the War still on!

I "took my time" – six months – meanwhile arranging for use of the Pigeon River Company's former office building across the track. It was frame but much more substantially built than my original shack and had a good heater.

Shortly after the real cold weather set in, Andrew, calling for his mail said, "Why for you not tell me station so cold place to live in?" What gratitude!

The only advantage of the change-over was that, freed of all responsibility to the railway company, I could sleep and have all meals at home. Since Vera's departure, Mother inevitably spent much of her time alone and although she was not in the least bit nervous, my greater freedom naturally pleased her.

Having always had great faith in insurance, I had tried every known agency to obtain protection against fire on all my buildings. Store and sawmill were definitely "out" owing to bushfire hazard, but by paying a very high premium I was able to protect the Bungalow.

Living at home also enabled me, during summer evenings, to pick and preserve the marvellous variety of wild fruit growing everywhere. Much to my surprise, I discovered that Toby was partial to the latter and would lead me to the best patches. These were of the larger variety and almost hidden by grass. Blueberries were found only on top of the mountain, gooseberries only on an island, necessitating a special trip. There were also red, white and black currants, the latter growing most profusely on the edges of creeks (roots practically under water), so wading was the easiest way to pick them. High and low-bush cranberries, even plums (rather rare) and thimble-berries were all available within reasonable walking distance.

It was never necessary to buy fruit for preserving,

except oranges for marmalade. And naturally we grew all our own vegetables. I even tried watercress, sowed under the drip of the eaves and transplanted to the creek.

I suppose it was owing to my position as Postmaster that all the registration jobs came my way. When an election was in the air, I'd be asked to arrange a meeting place for candidates and act as Deputy Returning Officer. Then, in later years of the War, came compulsory registration of residents. It happened when I was personally stacking the last carload of rough-edged lumber, and fortunately was close to my lock-up store. I could keep one eye on my work and the other on the arrival of groups of out-of-the-way registrants brought in by section-men on the railcarsthey used for going to and from work.

It was a strenuous Saturday, and on return home at 10 p.m. I said, "Please don't call me for breakfast. I feel like sleeping until noon." I was occupying what we called the summer bedroom, an addition to the Bungalow made necessary for the accommodation of guests.

About 8 a.m. I was awakened by a man's hoarse voice. "Miss Mitchell, the mill's burnt!"

"O.K. George, I'll be there in a few minutes."

Hastily dressing, I entered the house. Mother was astonished. "I thought you were going to sleep until noon?"

"So did I. But there's something wrong at the mill."

"Something wrong" was putting it mildly. The entire structure was destroyed and, because it had been built high above the creek, everything metal was utterly ruined, circular saws crumpled like tin foil. The engine, fortunately, was mounted on top of the boiler, which stood on solid ground and was still full of water. Although all the babbitt (a composite metal used in bearings to lessen friction) had run out of the engine, loss was not as acute as it might have been. On the other hand, a whole load of lumber had gone up in flames, because the teamster who would have been hauling it had to appear before the draft board in town.

Ironically, there was no bushfire in this instance. It had been deliberatly set, and I was morally certain who was the responsible party. But without evidence, nothing could be done, and I naturally kept my suspicions strictly to myself.

During the morning, people from all over the district came to view the remains. Several said, "Oh, you'll have to sell it for scrap. It will never pay to rebuild." With this, I did not agree, having several hundred logs already cut and lying in the bush, not to mention an unfulfilled contract.

I told my foreman to take measurements for all building material required (of necessity coming from city lumber yards, and costing three times as much as we could have produced it for), and I would order new circular saws and other equipment.

My gang, mostly local men, were naturally glad. All offered to work on reconstruction for a week, without pay.

Next day a Finn, whom I had never employed, came into the store and said, "You' mill burn? Me – my team – we work for you one week, no pay."

Even disaster has its compensations!

Mother's reaction, when she heard everything, over a delayed breakfast: "My dear, you're just like a rubber ball. The harder you're hit, the higher you bounce."

Rebuilding the mill was going to be a costly affair. It would have to be kept busy, so I'd better be looking for future contracts. Fortunately, poplar, worthless as either pulpwood, ties or cordwood, was in demand as lumber. On the homestead, it was diminishing but an adjoining mining-claim had still a quantity of poplar, after a recent cut of all the pine and spruce. This had been removed by a neighbour. If I asked him the name of the owner, he would probably think it a suggestion that he had been stealing the

stuff. So I wrote the Department of Mines and found the
lot was owned by a man living in Duluth. My offer was
promptly accepted, with the suggestion that I might find a
good market for lumber in his city; if I cared to go over, he
would gladly introduce reliable dealers.

Immediately after mailing a cheque for the agreed
amount, I sent men onto this lot to cut logs. The following
day, the chap who had previously removed the pine and
spruce, sent one of his boys over to ask who had given me
authority to cut on that particular lot. I smilingly rejoined,
''The owner.''

I made the suggested trip to Duluth, and it proved
most profitable. A big company offered a contract of up to
200,000 feet of special-dimension poplar at a price one-
third higher than could be obtained locally. It was to be 1
1/4 inches thick, and would be used for making shell boxes;
must be piled for a certain time to dry out and then shipped
to a firm in Hawkins, Wisconsin. Meantime they would
pay 50 percent, on the 10th of each month, on material
cut during the previous four weeks. Rather wonderful, I
thought, that they never sent over an inspector – just took
my word for the measure.

It was just around this time that Elizabeth, who had
become very friendly with Pierre's family, was one day
helping by scrubbing the kitchen floor, rough from long
usage without covering. A big sliver became lodged in a
finger of her right hand, proving very difficult to remove.
Hemlock, we were told, was sometimes poisonous and
had a habit of "slivering" both ways. Apparently most of
it remained embedded, but Elizabeth staunchly refused to
have it poulticed. "It'll fester," she insisted, "and the poison
will come out."

Instead, it got worse, the swelling and discolouration
spreading to the arm. I took her to the hospital, where, after

considerable unsuccessful treatment, the middle finger had to be amputated.

During convalescence, Elizabeth made herself so useful and popular in the children's ward, the Sisters persuaded her, as soon as she was able, to accept a position as nurse.

What Next?

The war was beginning to pose many problems, not the least being manpower, so essential to my business. Practically all the unmarried young men of the district had enlisted in the early days. There weren't many; of these, two had been killed shortly after reaching France, and two returned seriously disabled. Half the men in my logging-camp had quit, in order to join up.

Apart from enlistment of the men-folk, there was little we settlers could do in the matter of war effort except knit socks. I get the Red Cross Society to send up cartons of yarn, every woman being more than anxious to do her share.

I recollect, too, there was a tobacco company (was it Old Chum?) offering to send four packages of cigarettes to service men overseas, for every dollar subscribed, the donor being privileged to have his name and address on each package. Most people thought the scheme "fishy", though I did my best to aid it and took a chance myself. From three of the four recipients I received letters of thanks, one saying, "I've often been through Silver Mountain station when a brakeman for the C.N.R. And remember you well."

Walters had, of course, complete control of the gang working directly under him. I had never previously had occasion to employ men in any capacity and when this becomes necessary, decided the right way was to start out by telling them their duties and leave them to it. I avoided any interference unless work was unsatisfactory or they were abusing horses. That was taboo!

I'll admit that few took advantage of the situation, though a couple of instances come to mind. One was of a middle-aged man skidding logs. These were supposed to be "decked" on a couple of slim poles alongside the bush trails. One day, wandering around, I found him piling them in the middle of the road!

"Mr. Jones, (I always addressed older men as Mr.) that isn't the way to do it. How do you expect the teamster to load them onto the sleigh for hauling to the mill? He'll have to cut a road all the way around.

"Oh, well," he responded huffily. "perhaps you'd sooner get someone else to do it?"

"O.K. Put the team in the barn."

Walking over to the mill, I approached the foreman. "Do you think I could handle Keith's job? And let him skid logs."

"Why, yes. I guess you could. But what's happened to old Jones?"

"He got saucy when I told him the proper way to deck logs, so I suggested he put the team in the barn."

The other occasion was of a man hauling dry trunks of trees to the Bungalow, to be later sawed up for stove wood. To save himself trouble, he was making the team walk lengthwise of these trunks, which naturally caused them to slip and slide around. This might easily have resulted in a broken leg.

"George, I don't like the way you are handling the team."

He was a quarter-breed Indian, with incongruous china-blue eyes, and inclined to be blunt. Even so, his reaction was a bit starting: "Mebby you could handle 'em better yourself?"

"Maybe I could. But I'm in the middle of my dinner. Just tie them up to the fence." He skulked away, looking foolish.

There was already enough wood to last several weeks, and I had not the slighest intention of attempting the work.

(Sometimes I wondered if my training in mental nursing

was now helping me to deal with the many odd people encountered in this somewhat uncivilized part of the world. Assuredly, it taught one to make instant decisions!)

Immediately after dinner I hitched the team to the stoneboat to drive them to the farm. While heading for the track, their pace was leisurely, but the moment they found themselves directed towards the barn, they broke into a canter. It was all I could do to stay "aboard"! Indeed, finally, seeing a stump in direct line, I jumped and ran with them, rather than be thrown. Children and the handyman at the farm were all convulsed with laughter at what they termed my "circus act".

Keith's wasn't a hard job. As tail-sawyer, my duty was to take the boards as they came from the main saw, trim off the ends on the tail-saw, then slide them down to the loading zone at the end of the platform. I was definitely tired at the end of my first day as a mill-hand, but was compensated by the knowledge that I could fill in, at a pinch. It lasted only a few days, both the independent gentlemen coming back to seek reinstatement, doubtless at the instigation of their wives.

Sometimes city friends would say, "Why go further in to the wilds when taking a few days' holiday?"

Others – "Oh, I wish I lived up the Pee Dee! Something is always happening."

It was really a matter of taste. I loved this life.

Our local made only one trip weekly to North Lake, the terminus, 37 miles west of us. There I knew a most interesting family. The husband owned a large sawmill, and his wife and children, ranging in age from young men and women to infant, always made me welcome. I would take the in-betweens swimming, a great treat for them, nobody else having time and the shore rather treacherous. These youngsters loved to see me scramble onto a floating log and be promptly dumped; it takes much practice to acquire the art of "staying put".

The Railway had extended their telephone to the mill, so it was possible for us to keep in touch with one another. I kept them posted on war news, they told me of the latest addition. At times the baby arrived before the train, so Mama didn't go to the hospital; occasionally one of the girls would phone, saying they had run out of names for the fair sex. Could I suggest one?

I'd been told that a band of Indians might arrive at any time from Grand Marais, Minnesota, on their way to Whitefish Lake, to pick wild rice. But I did not see any until my second year in business. Then one day they flocked in, almost filling the store. Chief Black Jack spoke fairly good English, but took a keen delight in asking for things in the vernacular and watching me puzzle out the request. I soon discovered that one word with slightly different intonatin meant three or four things. Pa-meeta, for instance, applied to flour, bread or soda-biscuits. They had their own quaint way of doing business, too. Every item (even one plug of tobacco) was paid for individually, greatly prolonging the procedure. The Chief did his shopping first; then the other men. Next came the women, after which boys were given a little spending money, but girls got nothing. I had laid in a stock of rather gay prints, having been told this is what Indian women would prefer. Much to my surprise, they chose the more conservative colour and design. Of course I gave the small girls candy, and was able to get a rather nice snapshot of one of them, on the platform, with a neighbour's little girl. I wondered why sweet little Ida looked so scared. It transpired she had been told that if naughty, "the Indians would get her"!

As they were about to leave, the Chief said that if I lent him a gun, he would bring me some duck. This I did, and he bought two boxes of shells. A local customer came in just then and said "You don't expect ever to see your gun again, do you?"

But I thought they were honest, and sure enough, a few days later, in came Black Jack with the gun and four ducks.

I've wondered, on more than one occasion, if being located almost on the 90th meridian accounted for our having the most gorgeous display of Northern Lights. Often on what would have otherwise been a dark night, the heavens would be so illuminated by these constantly changing ephemeral forms – some like enormous fleecy wings, others moving islands – we would stand outdoors gazing until our necks were stiff. At times, it was possible to read by the glow.

Perhaps ur special geographical position was responsible for other "freaks'.

Earlier I mentioned a tornado that barely missed us. Violent electrical storms were not infrequent, but, as though to demonstrate what they could accomplish, the farm dwelling of a fine old Scottish couple was struck by a lightning bolt, which entered through the roof and penetrated two stories to the ground. One of their two adopted daughters, a very pretty girl of twenty-two, upstairs at the time, was close to the "strike". All her clothes and hair were burned from her and anything metal she had on her person was branded into her flesh. Furthermore, the poor girl was rendered blind and deaf. Tim Naylor immediately wired for a "special" – engine and coach – to convey Millie to the hospital. After a lengthy stay there, recovering from burns and shock, she mercifully regained her sight but not full hearing.

During this period, Tim became her devoted slave and literally showered gifts upon her. Eventually, Millie married him – out of sheer gratitude, we all felt, for they had never shown any interest in one another until after the tragic happening and had nothing in common. The house he chose in the city was a modest one, but lavishly furnished.

When the first baby (a boy) arrived Tim said firmly, "Now my Ma told me the right thing to do is to open the Bible, and put your finger on a page, without looking, and the first name you hit, is it!"

The proud daddy happened to hit Ishmael, and Ishmael the unfortunate child was named.

I called on Mrs. Tim soon after the second arrival. It was summer, the front door was stood open, so, remembering her slight deafness, I walked in and called, "Anyone at home?" From upstairs, she replied, "I'm just putting baby to rest. Be down in a few minutes."

Meanwhile Ishmael, not yet two, ushered me to a comfortable easy-chair, toddled over to a corner cabinet, from which he produced and solemnly presented to me a bottle of ale! By the time the mother appeared, the tot had paddled off to the kitchen. She laughed and said, "He's gone for an opener and a glass. Ishmael knows you won't drink it out of the bottle!"

Looking bright and happy, she remarked, during the course of the conversation, 'You know, I have everything in the world I want, except my own way. Tim won't allow me to correct Ishmael; he may do anything he wants – take my satin cushions out in the street – and I must not say a word. I'm afraid he'll regret it, sooner or later."

From all accounts, he did.

I lost sight of the Naylor family, when they moved to another district. The last I heard was of Tim's passing, in his late seventies. His mother had said he was "born to dance". What would she think, could she know he literally danced to his death? For he dropped dead in the middle of a backwoods square dance.

CHAPTER EIGHTEEN

Another Fire

It seems strange that people, finding themselves bearers of ill tidings, don't try to break the news gently.

After two particularly busy days in the city, winding up with a social gathering on the last evening, I felt like taking a surreptitous nap when settling into my seat on the Pee Dee train. Almost immediately, the baggage-master sat down beside me, saying bluntly, "Your store burned last night!"

Possibly, in time, one becomes shockproof in this part of our great Dominion. I was stunned for a moment; then said, "Last night? How can you know?"

"Andrew phoned down to Stanley and the Agent relayed the news to us."

"Seems to me strange, when the railway does not even own the building!"

Well, that was not the only strange thing about it, as I soon found on arrival at Silver Mountain. With only a few inches of smouldering rubble remaining, it was immediately evident that the place had first been robbed, then set afire. A light snowfall covered all footprints, but they wouldn't have been conclusive, anyway. The padlock on the door had been forced, the pieces dropped on the track. A metal despatch-box, in which I kept postal notes and stamps, was lying scattered in several pieces. There was no trace of whole sacks of flour and sugar, which would have just scorched in such a rapid blaze, not burned completely away. Also the metal containers in which I kept cereals were just not there. As to the fate of my lovely oak roll-top desk, a gift from Mother and Vera the previous

Christmas, no clue remained. It could have burned, but was more probably carted away. I could think only of two people in the district capable of such an act, and, without evidence, what could one do?

At Nolalu, on the way up from town, I had asked the Postmaster to notify the authorities of the fire and say that, if a new key were provided, I would receive and despatch mail until a new Postmaster could be appointed; at the same time I pointed out that my home was far from convenient for the purpose. Had not the railway company reverted to its original schedule the same day, I could not have attempted this offer of temporary mail service.

Here was a second instance where bush fires were not responsible for the conflagration. Not only did the stock represent a substantial monetary loss, but I later learned the postal authorities required me to make good all postal orders and stamps on hand.

Reaching the Bungalow, I was shocked to find that Andrew had gone up there in the middle of the night to tell poor Mother of the fire. How could any man be so heartless, knowing her to be elderly, a semi-invalid and alone! It could do no possible good, in any case. This, together with his notifying the Railway Company, set me wondering.

Mother and I naturally had a long and serious talk. This fire would cause far more complications than losing occupancy of the station had done. Was it being wished upon me to prove a blessing in disguise?

There was no knowing, with the war over and threat of depression in the air, how long timber contracts would be procurable. So I suggested it might be a good idea for me to find an apartment in the city, where Mother and Vera might make a home together. Although the matter had not been discussed, I'd felt for some time that Mother was anxious about the present arrangements. Vera, who was not strong, had room and breakfast in the home of very good friends, but it was some distance from the bank where she worked. This meant taking all other meals in restaurants – particularly awkward on holidays and Sundays – and she was not always getting the most nourishing of diets.

Mother heartily agreed with my idea, and when next visiting the city, I was fortunate in securing just what we wanted, the whole of the second floor (five furnished rooms) in a large converted home, only a couple of blocks from the Bank and near the Parish Church, which meant a good deal to them. Yes, in every respect, this seemed to be a wise decision. As soon as nearby timber was cut, it might be necessary to move the mill once more, and me with it!

For a while it seemed strange to again be a bachelor woman and sole occupant of the Bungalow, after having had one or both of my dear ones with me for nearly six years. However, I managed to keep busy all the time, sometimes fillling in at the mill, and felt quite flattered when one day Walters approached me and said:

"Do you think you could cut a new road for us – from the mill to the mine road? We're getting pretty well bogged down in mud-holes in the one we're using. But don't try to tackle any stumps you run into; I'll see to them, after work."

Cutting a road may seem, to the uninitiated, like a formidable undertaking. In this instance, I merely had to cut away all the brush and small trees for a width of about ten feet – and I'd already learned to handle an axe. Actually, I quite enjoyed it.

It is interesting to realize, in looking back, how often matters of importance seemed to resolve themselves. In checking up on avialable poplar for the contract on hand, I found it would be insufficient to complete the contract;

neither was there any more within hauling distance. It's a costly matter to move a mill; the regular gang, with extra help, dismantling, moving and setting it up again, all being paid wages and bringing no "income". Then along came a request from a lumber company in Duluth for a quantity of white pine lumber. There was still a large amount of this standing timber n the Fraleigh Limit, but it was impossible to take the mill there under existing road conditions.

Luck must have been with me, for I got permission to use an old mill site, about two miles down the track, where there was a short railway spur, and near the road leading out from the Limit. Not only this, but I had the use of an unoccupied log dwelling, just across the track, close by. This comprised a 1 1/2 storey house with a huge kitchen added at the back. On the ground floor there was a living room and two bedrooms, the whole layout requiring some rearrangement. This was accomplished during the mill-moving. I converted the kitchen into a bunkhouse for the men, and made one of the ground floor bedrooms into a kitchen. The upper storey, not yet partitioned, I made into three small bedrooms and an office. By the time all these arrangements were complete, October had brought the first snow.

But there were still two problems to be solved: obtaining a housekeeper and an outfit to cut and haul logs. In the first, could I find a city woman willing to work in this somewhat wild setting? There was, of course, no local person available. To my surprise, the first applicant said it was just what she would like, Her people had been among the first settlers at the Lakehead, then known as The Fort, shortly before she was born. She arrived, bag and baggage – just as a real cold snap had set in – escorted by her son-in-law, who took the first opportunity to whisper to me: "You won't keep her more than a week. We can't abide her around our place.”

What a cheering introduction! But, thank goodness, it was wrong. An excellent cook and bread-baker, she remained for nearly a year. Everyone called her “Grannie”, and I think she liked it. Probably I neglected to suggest that the old lady should leave her bedroom door partially open at night, so as to get greater benefit from the big heater. When retiring, she deposited her dentures in a glass of water which she placed on the window ledge. Next morning they were frozen in, solid! This wouldn’t have happened anywhere else in her room, because the ground floor was definitely warmer than the upper, as I found to my cost a few months later.

The coldest temperature I can remember was 52 degrees below zero and, happily, it lasted only about 24 hours. No outdoor work was attempted, and fires were kept going to capacity both in the camp and the mill boiler.

CHAPTER NINETEEN

Production Starts Again

The next important thing was to arrange for cutting and hauling from the Limit. Hearing of two men named Rendic in Fort William who might undertake this work, I arranged for them to come up and look over the proposition. The only man still living near who had worked for me several years ago on this Limit offered to act as a guide. Next morning the Rendics and I started real early, one of them carrying an ample lunch for the four of us, it being a five-mile hike each way, not to mention tramping around when we got there. Calling for Morton on the way, we found he was only just up, so had to wait while he had breakfast.

Our guide did not prove as good as anticipated, for at noon we hadn't sighted the timber we knew was somewhere near. I then said, "You men had better hunt around for dry wood and light a fire while Bambi and I climb this hill. The sandwiches will have to be thawed, you know."

Struggling up the mountainside through deep snow (Bambi almost buried, but game) I was rewarded by spotting on the other side the stand of timber we were looking for – and lots of it. On our return, a cheerful fire was blazing, the three men standing around, rubbing their hands and looking miserable or guilty – I wasn't sure which! It transpired that, while waiting for Morton to breakfast, the packsack containing the lunch had been laid on the floor and left behind.

As may be imagined, appetites were proportionately healthy when we reached camp! During the evening, details were discussed and a rate agreed upon, though at one point the elder Rendic became absent-minded and failed to respond to something I said. The younger dug him in the ribs with his thumb, remarking, "Miss Mitchell, she speak."

His response: "Oh, 'skuse me, lady! My think-attachment not working."

I then proceeded to draw up the contract, believing everything was now finalized, but they declined to sign until they'd seen their lawyer. Not only another delay, but it necessitated my going to town next day. After reading the document, the legal gentlemen handed it back to Rendic saying, "That's O.K. Miss Mitchell doesn't need a lawyer." I secretly thought they doubted the legality of the document because it was hand-written, instead of typed. But, reassured, they signed.

Work started almost immediately, and it was a comfort to have the mill running once more after the numerous delays. Everything went smoothly and uneventfully until one day, as we were all seated at dinner, someone jumped up, exclaiming, "Mill's afire!".

"Not again!" I moaned to myself.

We all dashed down the hill and formed a bucket-brigade. Luckily, it was just the roof covering the saw platform and was extinguished in short order. Sparks can do funny things, even in winter.

The builder of the house we were occupying had chosen to have the logs squared in a sawmill, instead of hewing the two sides, packing with moss and then "chinking" with plaster – making walls draught-proof. Obviously the timber had been used green and poplar contains a large percentage of moisture, so that every log shrank just enough to let air between, but not enough for chinking. On one occasion, when a strong west wind prevailed, paper was blown from

the walls, and I had to hang up blankets as protection.
Usually, I placed a hot-water bottle in the bed before
retiring, to take off the first chill. One morning, going up
to tidy my room after breakfast, I found the water frozen in
it! Through the night, I must have been keeping it warm.
And I had two winters of this; it's surprising what one can
accustom oneself to, if necessary.

As spring approached I bought a pig, which rapidly
became chummy with my collie, Bambi, and tried to
imitate his actions in many respects. Nigger, the cat,
would not even have his picture taken with the pair.
When neighbours' cattle attempted to trespass, Jocko (the
pig) would do his best to chase them away by zealously
snapping at their heels. Since a grunt was eminently
unsuccessful as a substitute for Bambi's bark, the intruders
took no notice, and Jocko's look of frustration was really
funny. Like children, the two would chase one another
around the sawdust pile; when Jocko found himself unable
to run fast enough, he'd scramble over the top and catch
up with Bambi. For a pig, I thought that pretty smart! Not
quite as versatile as my old friend Poke but still resourceful
for an animal generally supposed to be stupid. When he
learned the doggy trick of constantly jumping up at me,
wanting to be petted, he had to be more or less confined to
quarters.

Summer seemed to come early that year and Grannie
asked permission to have a small grandchild visit. Then
along came the wild fruit season. The old lady had several
cartons of sealers (plus 10 pounds of sugar) sent up to her
and spent all her spare time, and some that wasn't, picking
and preserving to take home. I'd always been in the habit of
having tea served to the men at 10 a.m. and 3 p.m. ("oiling
up" time). For this little duty Grannie was often missing,
either preserving or looking after Effie. Finally, hearing of

a couple who would like to come up, the wife as cook and
her husband cutting logs, I decided to dispense with the old
lady's services.

Somewhere around this time, Workmen's
Compensation came into being. Until its institution, it was
compulsory to deduct $1 per month from each employee,
pay this to a doctor whose duty it was to visit the camp
monthly and look after any that were hospitalized.

Rates on saw mills, because of above average
percentage of risks, were the highest imposed; yet I never
had occasion to put in a claim.

We were situated on a rate steep upgrade of the railway.
Consequently, trains never stopped at my spur coming from
town. If the conductor knew someone wanted to alight,
he'd give orders to slow down.

Things were running satisfactorily as far as the cook-
log-cutter combination was concerned, but the engineer,
for family reasons, found it necessary to quit, though
considerately giving me time to find a replacement. Being
very patriotic, I instructed the Employment Bureau to send
only returned men. First to arrive was a fellow who firmly
refused to go down and light the boiler fire before breakfast
(a one-minute walk) because he "was only supposed to
work nine hours a day". This meant there was no steam
until mid-morning, the rest of the gang hanging around
with nothing to do. He didn't last long!

The second said that, firing with green wood kept
him so busy, he hadn't time for a smoke; he quit of his
own accord. The third, a smartly dressed young fellow,
dropped off the train with two swanky leather suitcases.
I took him to be a traveller. Informing me that he was the
new engineer, he requested that I have his trunk brought
down from the station, because he couldn't start without his

work clothes. A team couldn't be spared until evening, so someone lent him a suit of overalls; he still wore his stiff white "choker" collar! I didn't believe he had ever handled such a job before. After two days I called the foreman in. "I'm getting fed up with these so-called engineers! We're not even making expenses, Mr. Walters. I've a notion to tackle it myself."

"Well, Ma'am, you can do anything else around the mill, so I don't see why not, if I show you the workings."

"Then that's settled; and if I'm as useless as these men we've been getting, I'll close down."

It was a little exaggeration to say I could "do anything else around the mill". I had tried my hand as top-sawyer, but the 'knowing how' was not enough; I couldn't possibly handle the logs which often required two men to turn on the carriage.

It was strenuous work, and I fear that for the first few days steam wasn't quite up to standard, although I stoked up every twenty minutes, using about a cord and a half of wood daily. This was composed of slabs and edgings from the logs (all green, of course) cut to suitable length by the tail-saw, located just within the wall of the boiler house. Everything fell in a heap below this small saw, and in between whiles I would carry my fuel over and pile it close to the fire-box. I don't think it was exactly hard work. More probably intense heat coming from the furnace while stoking caused me to lose 13 pounds weight in the first two weeks. I had to tie a large handkerchief around my forehead to prevent perspiration running down my face! One day, throwing in an armful of edgings, one of them jumped back and broke my glasses. Shortly after, one of the gang happened to come in and exclaimed:

"What have you been doing to your face, Miss Mitchell?"

"Nothing that I know of. Why?"

"Well, it's just streaming with blood!"

What a narrow escape. Glasses versus eye.

I've always been very sensitive to sound where machinery is concerned. If anything unusual is audible, I want to know what it is.

The drive-belt – 11 inches wide and of solid leather – would be about twenty feet long, running from the engine to main shaft. On one occasion I kept hearing a light, periodic "tap" at the far end of the boiler room, so, armed with a big monkey-wrench, I climbed around to test the boxings holding the shaft. I hated to shut down until I'd at least tried to locate the trouble! Well, the boxings were as tight as clams. I'd just decided to call the foreman, and had my hand on the throttle to shut off the engine when the whole belt broke loose, flying with tremendous force towards the spot on which I'd been standing a few seconds earlier, crashing against the end of the building. Walters hurried in, his face blanched, thinking there had been an explosion. It transpired that the "lacing" holding the two ends of the belt together had gradually loosened, and it was one end hitting part of the machinery that I had heard.

Even had I been killed, as I almost assuredly would if hit by that terrific force, nothing could have been claimed from the Workmen's Compensation Board. I was not a certified engineer and had no right to be on the job!

However, I carried on for a total of nearly three months, and had only one other notable experience. I always wore heavy horse-hide gloves, with gauntlets, while working, and was one day standing on the pile of cut-off slabs, gathering an armful to carry over to the fire-box. Suddenly my left foot slipped, and I fell with my right hand on the small circular saw – going full speed. Two fingers of the glove were neatly sliced through! I'm sure I gazed for a full minute before removing it, fully expecting the tops of two fingers would remain within. One was badly cut, the other bruised where it had been jammed on the frame. I wrapped up the bleeding one in a handkerchief and continued working. But the bruise was so very painful, I shut down. "I'm going up to the house, Mr. Walters," I said, "to put something on this jammed finger."

"Oh," said he, "I've got a lot better remedy than anything you have at the house," and he proceeded to gather up gum that was oozing from white-pine logs on the skid-way and plaster it onto the injury. Sure enough, the pain ceased almost immediately. He had probably learned this trick from the Indians, so versed in all nature remedies.

CHAPTER TWENTY

Camp Cook

I can't say I exactly regretted it when a capable engineer came along and offered his services; Walters had known him in the past and vouched for his reliability. It was pleasant to once again live a "life of leisure" and have time for at least a fleeting visit to the city. On one of these occasions, the train agent said, "Miss Mitchell, if you've time, the Superintendent would like you to drop in and see him."

I did, rather wondering what it could be about. It appeared that one of the city lumber companies wished to load cars on my spur. They had informed the railway company that at the time of its being put in for another man to load a quantity of logs they had a half-interest in it.

"Strange they've never questioned my using it," I said. "May I see that agreement?" This was handed to me. It was signed by their yard foreman and looked like a "cooked up" job to suit their present requirements.

"That may have been so, several years ago. But since I have paid the rent for the past two years, you may tell the Company they can load cars – at my convenience, and by paying the small fee that I charge any settler who requires the privilege. They don't even own any timber in that area, and I'm quite sure that if they'd have any legal rights, they would have charged me for using the spur." I never heard another word on the subject.

Returning from those few restful days with the family, I felt braced for anything, as the saying goes. Nothing unusual happened for about a week. Things were working smoothly, both in mill and camp. But Fate decreed that my leisurely life be of short duration. Suddenly it happened.

The housekeeper's husband finished his log-cutting job, refused a monthly one and the couple left without a day's notice. What a predicament! I was considered a fairly good cook, but to be suddenly faced with the necessity to feed six hearty men and one always-hungry boy was startling. Meat and vegetables would be no problem, and though rather dreading the endless procession of pies and cakes, I felt capable of handling the job – with one exception. I did not know how to bake bread.

A neighbouring farmer's wife promised to do this for me until I could have some sent from the city. (It came fourteen loaves to the sack.)

Hearing of my predicament, one of the mill-gang, a French-Canadian and father of the sixteen-year-old lad, Joe, came to me and said, "My boy, 'e learn you 'ow! Me, I 'ave raise now ten chil'n and w'en my missis she 'ave baby.... Joe mak' bread."

Well, the first batch was handled by Joe "in toto", with a running accompaniment of advice to me as he proceeded. The second, I undertook, with him standing by. This turned out topnotch, much to our mutual delight.

Next morning, Joe rather shyly handed me written instructions (lest I forget, presumably), pencilled on a soiled leaf torn from a notebook.

"Take potato water One pine Ad 1 tabl spoon salt 1 cup flowr wen worm have one yeast cake disolv in worm water ad that to potato water. set itill it workes. Flowr one hand ful. Ad salt. put luck worm water of required. not to stiff. set aside to rise til mornin then beet down two times then put it in panes let it raise then bake it about one oure."

I still treasure this masterpiece of a recipe. To me,

it symbolized Joe's devotion to his mother – everything he did was with a smile – and his own lack of schooling consequent on the nine younger "chil'ns".

Many people are under the impression that a porcupine has the power to actually eject and throw its quills. This is entirely erroneous. The quills are loosely inserted in the animal's skin, and become embedded in the flesh of the attacker.

More than once, I've had to use pliers to draw quills out of our dogs' faces. Although it must have been a painful process, they would sit absolutely docile, apparently aware they were being helped. The fact that the tip is barbed and furnished with many reversed points or prickles accounts for the difficulty in removing them. Sometimes the tip breaks off and works inward, causing ulcers.

Bambi showed marked intelligence. On his second scrap with a porcupine, he apparently remembered the first painful experience. This time, he just patted it with one paw, then came ambling home on three legs, the quilly paw held high. This happened at my sawmill camp one Sunday afternoon. All the men were awy, strolling or visiting, except old Walters. After shooting the creature, I asked him to bury it.

"Oh, no, ma'am!" he protested. "That's mighty good eating. I'll skin it for you."

It weighted fourteen pounds, before skimming and cleaning. After jointing, I put it in brine overnight (the correct procedure for all four-legged wild meat), then stewed it with onions, a few leaves of dried sage, some lemon rind and two tablespoonsful of mushroom ketchup. Later the gravy was thickened. It made a truly appetizing dish, the flesh being light in colour and in flavour a cross between pork and turkey.

The men obviously enjoyed the meal but were too polite to ask what they were eating. They of course knew, from the size of the joints, that it wasn't rabbit but later the subject came under discussion in the bunkhouse. Next morning Walters confided to me, a mischievous twinkle in his eye, "They've decided it was beaver-meat, and you didn't mention it because beaver is out of season."

This really made a pleasant change of menu, since in summer meat must be either smoked or salt variety, varied occasionally by fish.

Certainly, I'd never before realized how eager these hard-working men were for pies; they would have welcomed them even for breakfast, I feel convinced. Having them twice daily, it was difficult to ring the changes. Then a brilliant idea struck me. "Pumpkin, of course! All Canadians love pumpkin pie."

By this time, I'd lived in Canada for fifteen years, and had yet to meet a British-born person who might be said to even mildly enthuse over this all-American delicacy. A few acquire the taste. Others, never!

Personally, I've always felt somewhat ashamed of my initial encounter with pumpkin pie, knowing it to be a highly-thought-of-dish of my adoptive country.

I'd been in Toronto only a few months when offered the position of assistant to the Manageress of a large private hotel. This lady, Miss Strang, I had met aboard ship, coming out. The proprietors, also British, lived on the premises, but considered it "infra dig" to take any hand in the management. They had one little girl and the little girl had a governess.

Grace Hilton, the governess, and I became friends, spent our very limited leisure together and naturally compared impressions of this New Country. One custom we considered rather barbarous as having Sunday's evening meal at 5.30 and nothing thereafter until Monday's breakfast. After a fairly long walk to and from Church, we returned from Evensong with ravenous appetites. On learning of this, Miss Strang gave me a key to the pantry, telling me to take anything I found there.

My first exploratory invasion was not too productive. Part of a pie, whose nature I could not determine, promised the most substantial "snack", so I cut two sizab le helpings and donveyed them to my room, three flights up.

I waited while Grace took the first taste.

"How is it?" I asked.

"Well, I can't say I like it; but I'm hungry enough to eat anything!"

It was my turn now to sample it.

"Oh!" I exclaimed. "It's simply horrible! I can't taste anything but spices, and they're all jumbled up!"

"What are you going to do with it?" queried Grace, practically. "You can't put it in the wastepaper basket. And if you return it to the pantry, you'll mortally offend the chef."

"And what's more, " I added, "the kitchen is locked, or it could go down the garbage-chute."

Grace's next suggestion indirectly solved the problem. "How about putting it in a paper bag, taking a walk and quietly 'straying' it? Some dog will spot it in no time."

"Dogs!" I exploded. "You've given me a brilliant idea. I'll just throw the pie out of the window, and presto!... it will be gobbled up immediately."

It so happened there was a ten or twelve foot lane between the hotel and a large church. I opened the window side and threw the offending slab of pie, apparently with too much force. It struck the wall of the church, gooey side first, and stayed there! Worse still, it stayed there for a matter of ten days, and there was nothing I coudl do about it but feel horribly ashamed.

Yes, that was my first encounter, and for a long time afterwards I strenuously avoided experimenting with any unkonwn specimen of the genus gourd. Now, on this seconed (and unpremeditated) encounter, the catch was – no pumpkin.

I'd never heard of substituting but decided on an experiment. In the root-house were some particularly mild Swede turnips. Out came the cookbook, and after scanning the recipe, I was convinced that my somewhat satirical appellation of All-American "dainty" was not far wrong. It seemed that for two pies, one must use, in addition to the basic ingredient, 3 cups of scalded milk (a little cream being an improvement), 1 1/2 cups of brown sugar, small portion of butter, 1/4 teaspoon salt, 3 eggs (whites and yolks beaten separately) and 1 1/2 teaspoons of ginger, cinnamon, cloves and nutmeg. The completed pie to be topped with meringue.

With the exception of my substitute, I followed the recipe meticulously – with unqualified success.

Every one of the seven participants (yes, even the cook!) voted them the "best pumpkin pies ever!"

There was at least one advantage accruing from my promotion to Camp Cook. I inherited the privilege of occupying the ground floor bedroom, which was infinitely more comfortable than the upper one.

Not long after this, a man was seen walking down the track, wearing – what was quite unusual – a long overcoat, instead of the customary short mackinaw. When abreast the mill he stopped, looked alternately at it and the camp, as though uncertain what to do. Presently he accosted a teamster, saying he wanted to talk to Walters, who was a

friend of his. Since he refused to go down to the mill, the
foreman came to the track.

"Hello, Larry, heading for home?"

"I don't know ...you got a gun?"

"No. Why?"

"I want you to shoot me."

Walters, knowing that the fellow was more than a trifle
deranged, humoured him by saying, "Well, I'll see if I can
borrow one. Meantime, you'd better come down to the
boiler-house and warm up."

All this was repeated to me later, with the suggestion
that I let Larry remain for a few days, while we notify
the authorities of his whereabouts. "He's a bit screwy,
but harmless. You see, there's no mental institution in the
Twin Cities, and he's been allowed to stay with another
friend, who runs a camp about 11 miles further up the line.
Evidently he's run away."

"Sure he can stay, if you'll keep an eye on him."

That evening (as I later learned) Larry had threatened
to go outdoors and "get frozen". Wearing neither coat,
shoes nor socks, he rolled up his sleeves above the elbow
and trousers above the knee, and left the sleep-camp to
brave the 38 degrees below. But it wasn't long before he
returned – to warm himself at the big box-stove. The rest of
the men treated the occurrence as a joke. To me, it wasn't
a bit funny. While they were all at work next day, I entered
their quarters and commandeered all the razors. While
glad enough to help the poor fellow, I didn't relish the idea
of a suicide on the premises! After a few days, Larry's
brother came and took him away – something of a relief to
everyone.

I'd quite enough on my mind, just then, without such
extraneous matters. With no contracts in sight beyond
the Duluth one we were engaged on, I had to face the

possibility of a shutdown. If it came to that, what would I do about the mill? I couldn't just sit there and keep an eye on it; neither could I afford a paid watchman. It was more than likely that all moveable parts would be stolen.

Then the almost unbelievable happened. A former mill owner came along and wanted to buy mine; said it had the reputation of producing the best lumber on the Pee Dee. My personal opinion was that Walter's meticulous attention to detail was responsible – not the mill itself – but I didn't argue the point. Furthermore, the price offered was slightly above what I had originally paid for it; the remainder of the contract on hand I threw in as a bonus.

It took only a short time to dispose of surplus furniture at the Bungalow, and have the rest of our possessions packed and shipped to storage in Port Arthur until I could buy a suitable home for the three of us there. So ended my twelve years' pioneering in the "bush" – years I have never regretted, despite periods of heartbreak, which were more than compensated for by the intense interest of varied experiences and the lifelong friends I made there. I still keep in touch with some in their 90s!

CHAPTER TWENTY-ONE

The Later Years

So now, at 44, I was about to start life all over again. None of the occupations in which I had become fairly proficient during twleve years in the wilds would be of any use in the city, excepting bookkeeping. Of this, necessarily, I had learned a good deal, and although the accuracy of my figures had won two lawsuits, the methods employed could hardly be called strictly orthodox.

On moving to Port Arthur, I naturally joined Mother and Vera in their apartment, and immediatley decided to take a course at business college, studying everything but shorthand which I felt would be too monotonous. Upon graduation, the Principal asked me to remain as relief-teacher while the regular staff took their vacations. This I thoroughly enjoyed.

Mother was a gifted director, so the three of us put in our spare time organizing and producing concerts and plays to raise funds for Church and other organizations. Meantime, we were on the lookout for a home – of appropriate size, price and locality – which I might buy. At length a possible one appeared on the horizon, a seven-room, solidly constructed frame dwelling, well up on a hill.

Not immediately seeing a permanent position to my liking, I continued to "fill in" on temporary ones. The first was in the accounting (freight) office of the C.P.R. in Fort William during the Lakehead's annual rush of grain from the West for storage in elevators. Rather strenuous, since it meant leaving home at 7.30 each morning, walking some distance to a street-car, and often wading through deep snow and climbing a long flight of unswept steps to each

the office – in the midst of shunting yards. Arrival even
a few minutes past 8.30 meant being docked half-a-day's
pay! If my memory serves me, cars of grain were coming in
at the rate of fifteen hundred a day.

Next, over the especially busy Christmas season, came
a session of "pinch hitting" for the bookkeeper-cashier of a
large men's clothing store. My office was a sort of elevated
platform at the rear, from which I had to make change
for cash sales and "on accounts". Little containers came
dashing toward me on a system of elevated rails and wires
and the important thing, I found, was to take them in proper
sequence! This was a six-weeks job.

So far as I recollect, I never applied for any position
I held nor business I acquired during those 23 years in
Port Arthur. Sometimes, it must be admitted, acceptance
was a matter of expediency; at others, appointments were
practically forced upon me. Something always was turning
up to open new doors of experiences.

There came an offer from a chartered accountant just
opening an office of his own. He had graduated, as well,
in law at Oxford. I naturally foresaw excellent experience.
During the early days, my employer was perforce out a
good deal, stirring up business, while I, in order to look
busy when anyone called, would be rattling full speed on
the typewriter – composing short stories. Sometimes my
boss would come in, dump a pile of books on the high
desk and say, "Mr. So-and-So would like a profit and loss
statement for the past six months", and walk out. This was
responsibility I would never have been given in a larger
firm.

After about eighteen months, when things were really
flourishing, another clerk was hired. Our successful
employer then began spending his afternoons at his Club
and part of the mornings recovering from "the night

before". Finally, he left the city – deeply in debt. Most of the clients offered me their business if I would open an office of my own. At first thought, such a venture seemed fantastic. However, I decided to try it, combining accountancy with real estate. Depression following the First World War had not yet subsided, so affairs in real estate were slack, chiefly collecting rents and mortgage payments, with an occasional sale. Sometimes, too, it was possible to buy a small property, make improvements and either rent or sell on easy terms. This sparked the purchase of my first car – a very second-hand Chevrolet. Family and friends, during off-duty periods, had many adventures though "Pegasus" never came to actual disaster.

This venture continued for about six years, during which period (in 1929) I found relaxation in helping to form the Amateur Cinema Society of Port Arthur. This involved writing the scenario for their first production, "A Race for Ties", a comedy-drama. The plot was based on happenings in Chapter VIII of "Lady Lumberjack", but substituting a young girl as heroine and of necessity altering some incidents.

A very sad time followed, when I lost my dear Mother and sister Vera within fifteen months of one another. Now there was less motive for the daily grind of work. After persistent urgings by relatives in Southern California to come and live among them, I decided to do so. I sold my business and most of my personal possessions, leased the home for a year and was all prepared for the move, when once more Fate stepped in to decide my course.

The Board of Governors of the new General Hospital offered me the position of secretary-treasurer. Would I go out to meet the Superintendent and members of the Board on a certain afternoon? Although firmly determined to decline the honour, it seemed only courteous to accede to their request. The new Superintendent was a Scottish-American woman and, as I later discovered, a real martinet. It seemed the lady absolutely refused to have a man in the office and insisted upon an entirely new system of bookkeeping. I hardly consider it a compliment that the hospital board wanted me; there just wasn't another woman accountant in the district. Well, I attended as requested; told them I was definitely going to California to live, even had my visa, so could not possibly consider their offer. A week later, another interview was requested. This time, determined to "choke them off" by telling them that, in any event, I would require a much higher salary than they had been paying – nearly double – an amount I had been offered in California. This rather staggered them. Then the chairman suggested calling a meeting of the whole board to discuss the matter and I returned home with the feeling, "that's that!". Meantime, their auditors were consulted. Those worthies said that, if I were on the job, the difference in salary would be more than compensated for by their lower fees.

It truly began to look as though Fate had a hand in my staying in Canada. Rather reluctantly, I accepted. It was then I was told they could not afford to give me an assistant, that I would have some additional duties. It turned out that I was expected to operate the switchboard, admit patients and have charge of charts! I was to earn my good salary. I forget the exact number of beds, but the Hospital was six storeys and ultra modern. Often I worked from nine in the morning until midnight, but was eventually given a stenographer. After about fifteen months, just after return from my first annual vacation, I was politely informed that "now things were running smooothly, the Board felt they could get someone at a lower salary."

By this time, slightly fed up with jobs in general, I

decided to take leave of regular duties and live in a five-room bungalow I owned on the outskirts of town and spend my time improving it. The biggest item was laying hardwood floors (oak shorts) in dining and living room: somewhat tedious, including sanding, varnishing and waxing, but well worth the effort.

Next spring I was offered the job of running the office of an insurance agency, the owner having acquired a municipal position in the same building. All I knew about insurance was through experience in real estate. However, things went along satisfactorily for some two-and-a-half years, when the owner planned moving to Toronto. Would I consider buying the agency? Since, at that time, I seemed to be the only female in either insurance, real estate or accountancy, I first wrote all the thirteen Companies we represented, asking if they would have any objection to the takeover. They were all agreeable, and the Mitchell Agency ran along for another two years, when I sold the business, deciding to retire on a small annuity and revenue from properties acquired. This change enabled me to spend most of the winter in California. On return to the Lakehead, my time became pretty well occupied in volunteer work. Besides intensive training in the Red Cross Transport Corps with written exams in a number of subjects, I was on the executive of Church organizations, Daughters of the Empire, the Humane Society, Camera Club and I formed a group for the British Waifs and Strays. In the fall of 1939, I was in charge of Voluntary Registration of Canadian women and assisted the Children's Aid Society in placing British child guests in city and district.

In 1942 I was talked into yielding up my much-interrupted retirement once more. This time, it was a paid Government job as secretary to the Dependents' Advisory Board. It was intensely interesting work.

When I came to retire again – this time on recommendation of my doctor – and to move to Victoria, B.C., I had over 1800 cases on file from dependents of servicemen.

During those 23 years of city life, holidays were varied. When time was limited, I'd choose some restful spot, not reachable by phone, either in the Lakehead region or Northern Minnesota. Later, during attempts at retirement, I would drive to California or Toronto – sometimes for the winter. Once I spent a most enjoyable vacation in the North West Territories with old friends; another, by rail in Maryland, Washington, D.C. and Staten Island. And last, but not least, I owned a charming little island, on an inland lake, 18 miles from Port Arthur. This retreat was a constant joy.

*   **

Sometimes I wonder if many parents realize that a sense of balance – both mental and physical – will help their youngsters in later life. It engenders the ability to "stay on top" when everything around seems to be slipping away; to weigh good against evil (even in one's associates) and to calmly accept the medium; to remain composed, even under the most trying circumstances.

One of my earliest recollections is of being taught to be afraid of nothing. I'm quite sure my Mother herself was fearless, or she wouldn't have allowed us to ride half-wild ponies, swim in strange waters and climb dangerous cliffs. Possibly she was disappointed at having no sons, which might account for her letting us, two girls, learn carpentry under the direction of the parish Clerk and Undertaker. I remember being fascinated by the construction of coffins, and decided I'd like to make my own. However, having

147

ambitions to travel, I later decided it might be a nuisance to carry around.

This somewhat "unladylike" ability to handle carpenters' tools certainly stood us in good stead! Vera and I built bookcases, cupboards, a chest of drawers and even a divan. For the latter, we bought a 27-inch wide bedspring and mattress, built quite professional-looking ends, and upholstered the matteress with some old family tapestry. This frequently was used as extra sleeping accommodation.

Obviously the local people thought us a big odd because we could walk the length of a log – often elevated – without any difficulty, whereas even the men wouldn't attempt it unless wearing calked boots. Our youthful admiration for the travelling circus had inspired in us the determination to do a tight-wire act in our own garden. Naturally we had no means of tightening the wire when suspended between two trees; and a slack wire is infinitely more difficult to perform on. Just the same, we persevered until we could not only walk it, but turn around and kneel on the wire, picking up an article placed there. This led to walking the top rail of fences when out in the country. There were no ice rinks where we lived, but roller-skating was popular, and – I'm inclined to think – helped us to keep upright on icy roads made exceptionally smooth by sleigh-runners. Neither of us looked particularly athletic nor robust; my height was 5 feet 7 1/2 inches and average weight 138 pounds.

After about three years at Silver Mountain, Vera felt restless and decided to accept a position offered her by the Bank of Montreal. She naturally spent all her holidays with us, frequently bringing along a friend. On one such occasion, the two decided to take a walk along the river bank to view the falls. For this, they crossed the only nearby bridge and followed the trail along the far side.

The afternoon wore on with no sign of their return, so I set out to look for them, taking my gun and a length of rope in case they were either held up by some probably harmless wild creature, or had slipped down the sometimes steep embankment – and couldn't get up! Their footprints could be seen going in patches of unmelted snow, but none returning. With dusk approaching, I decided to go back for a lantern, and possibly help. Entering the Bungalow, there sat the three of them (Mother and the two girls) gaily eating their supper!

"How on earth did you get back?" I demanded. "There isn't another bridge for miles."

"Oh, we found a big tree that had fallen across the river. I walked it, and Amy followed on hands and knees."

"Yes," chimed in that lady, "and you can't imagine how terrified I was!"

Another thing which puzzled the settlers was our ability to walk long distances without tiring. This was not one of the fads we had deliberately taken up; it came about in this way.

When in our early teens, we attended a class in National Dancing, conducted by an old gentleman (at least we thought him old!) one Captain Ian McCuaig, a tall, wiry Scot, who had been known as the best Highland dancer in the Queen's Own Edinburgh Regiment. Posture was what he emphasized at every turn – not only in dancing, but in walking. "If the shoulders are kept in line with the ball of the foot, one should never tire!".

Because he was a bachelor, and living alone, a standing invitation to Sunday dinner was issued, after which it was customary for us to accompany the Captain on long walks into the country – at his favourite pace of four miles per hour! This was strenuous for girls (even with correct posture) and we occasionally gained respite by throwing a stick into the woods for our dog to retrieve. However,. The habit stayed with us through life.

But what really worried these people (women especially) was my walking fairly long distances, after dark, alone. Arguing the point didn't seem to do much good. I'd say, "What are you afraid of?"

"Oh, there are wild animals – bears and wolves – in the bush."

"Have you, or has anyone you know, been attacked by these animals?"

They had to admit they had never heard of such an event.

Some thought it very brave to live alone in such uncivilized territory. I'd quash this by saying: --

"If I were afraid, it would be very brave; but, you see, I'm not!"

Which reminds me of a little incident during my early days in the Station. One evening a man came in to buy tobacco, then went over to the Pigeon River office, where a group of men were playing poker. A violent thunderstorm came up, and this man (not wanting to join in the game) said, "I think I'll go over and see if Miss Mitchell is afraid of the storm." One of the players – a Canadianized American – exclaimed, "That wumman! She's a-skeered of nawthing!". Some of my best compliments came to me second-hand!

Looking back, too, I see many little things I had not time to notice then. In all those twelve years, I was never addressed by my first name. This may have arisen from the fact that I was the only person employing local labour; which made it advisable to show respect! Neither did I ever apparently warrant a nickname, as nearly everyone else did. (The term "Lady Lumberjack" originated among city associates). Nor, despite frequent manly occupations, did I wear masculine garb except on horseback.

I must have received at least eight proposals of marriage – two by proxy (these were from oddities) – and two in such outlandish language, I didn't realize the implications until suddenly finding myself engaged! When I first struck this strange part of the country, I was the only single woman between the ages of 16 and 40, a fact which could hardly be ignored. Then there was the general impression, because I had good contacts and was busy all the time, that I was making piles of money; no one seemed to consider the heavy losses suffered through fires, crooked deals, bad weather holding up work and keeping teams and men idle. But in at least two instances my apparent success could have inspired matrimonial interest.

***

In retrospect, I am grateful for the kind of life and opportunity I found in Canada. The vagaries of fate seemed to intermeddle in my life and circumstances dictated that over the years there would be many variations and interests involved in the ncessary business of making a living in this good, adopted land. But of all the times, the "boss lumberjack" days were best. Perhaps much of the satisfaction of it came from the fact that I, a mere female, was able to survive in what was certainly a man's world long before an executive in skirts had come to be a phenomenon that was accepted as only slightly unusual.

Other days, other ways – and these are other days when a woman is not regarded as an oddity if she expresses in practical affairs some talent for getting things organized and under way. The converted stationhouse, the mill, the family life that somehow was richer for the very fact of being in a degree of isolation, are memories now but pleasant to revive.

The setting down of these events may serve to do little more than satisfy the ever-present urge to write that went with me from earliest childhood. It is an account of a period in Canadian history when anyone with the will to work and with a spark of enterprise could find himself – or herself – caught up in the task of pushing back the frontier in the country west of the Great Lakes.

And, incidentally, the reason this book exists at all is because the son of the Big Boss of Silver Mountain Mines – himself an author – would not cease his urging until I had taken to pen and typewriter in a commitment to put the story, so to speak, on the record.

Appendix

To the younger generation, this chronicle of life on the famous little Pee Dee may sound like a myth. For their benefit, it can be mentioned that the Pee Dee was originally known as the Thunder Bay Colonization Railway. It was opened to traffic in 1893, nine years prior to completion of the C.N.R.'s main line from Port Arthur to Winnipeg. Later it became known as the Port Arthur, Duluth and Western, but got no farther than Gunflint on the International Boundary, the American line failing to connect. The cost of this branch line is said to have been $1,296,000 – a lot of money in those days!

Owing to the fabulous production of the Silver Islet Mine, credited with an output worth two-and-a-half million dollars in its earlier years, Port Arthur became known as the "Silver Gateway".

Practically all the Pee Dee ore discoveries are credited to Oliver Daunais (born in St. Ours, Quebec 1837). Coming west, he had worked for a while at the Silver Islet Mine; then began exploring the mainland in a westerly direction. Notable among Daunais' discoveries were several on the Rabbit Mountain Range – the Beaver, Porcupine, Rabbit and Silver Creek – in addition to the East and West End Mines at Silver Mountain, the latter by far the richest in production. It is believed that these are all on the same vein of silver ore as the Silver Islet, although the West End is around fifty miles distant and 300 feet above the level of Lake Superior. Oliver Daunais, understandably, earned for himself the title of "Silver King".

Gradually over the years 1916 to 1938, one-time extensive mining and lumbering operations ceased. The more westerly section was dismantled in 1923. Fifteen years later, all rail activities came to an end, with the exception of the first 12 miles from the city, this portion becoming part of the C.N.'s Kashabowie Subdivision.

But the good old Pee Dee was still capable of "doing her bit", tracks were torn up to be used in the manufacture of munitions during World War II.

Silver Mountain Rises

Shelley Simon at Silver Mountain Station.

Photo by Elle Andra-Warner.

Born in Windsor, Ontario, I lived and grew up in Cottam, Ontario. After my first culinary job at the *Leamington Dock Restaurant* in Leamington, I continued in the hospitality industry and in 1996, joined the *Windsor Casino*, working in various positions until openings in the culinary department became available when the casino was renamed *Caesars Windsor*. In May 2010 the opportunity in Northwestern Ontario came my way and I moved to Silver Mountain, Ontario to begin a new journey at the Silver Mountain Station.

I opened the Station as an ordinary restaurant, eventually learning about the building's history and about Dorothea Mitchell. I was intrigued by the significant Canadian history that had taken place at Silver Mountain, most particularly by this iconic woman who had spent so much time here. Her significant role as an extremely astute business woman in a man's world, and all that she accomplished in her life, fascinated me. Reprinting her book Lady Lumberjack was a must.

The Silver Mountain Station Restaurant is now a historic destination, housed in the only remaining railway station on the former Port Arthur, Duluth and Western Railway. One can still feel the spirit of Dorothea Mitchell within its walls.